PRINTED IN THE UNITED STATES OF AMERICA

Copyright © 2013 Straightline Publishers, LLC
Library of Congress Control Number: 2013934120
ISBN: 978-0-9824746-3-1

TheSmartestWay™
TO
SAVE MORE

TheSmartestWay™

TO

SAVE MORE

Making the Most of Your Money

Samuel K. Freshman & Heidi E. Clingen

TheSmartestWay™ to Save More

Making the Most of Your Money

By Samuel K. Freshman and Heidi E. Clingen

FIRST EDITION
Straightline Publishers, LLC
"The Shortest Distance to Your Goal™"
Los Angeles, California, USA

Visit our website and sign up for free tips at
www.TheSmartestWay.com

Email us at
Heidi@TheSmartestWay.com

What Readers Say About
TheSmartestWay™ to Save More, Making the Most of Your Money

"If you really want to save, after reading this book, there is no way to not succeed. Because of the current economy, the best thing anyone of us can do is to cut back without cutting out, and this book can certainly help you to achieve that goal!"

—Chaplain Anne Bowman, M.S.
Lifetime Teaching Credential

"Practical and reasonable, this book is a useful book that guides readers toward a more frugal lifestyle without sacrificing quality. Whether the topic is using coupons more effectively or modifying online spending habits, this book is ready to assist with useful advice that helps consumers reign in unnecessary spending and improve overall financial health."

—Bryan Carey,
Owner of www.MoneySavingParent.com

"In Sam and Heidi's first book, I discovered how to change my spending habits and create, as I would an art form, a system of self-discipline that now helps me live without the stress of debt and within my means. Their second book has essential "next steps" to save whenever and wherever I can—from couponing to clothes shopping, dining out, even gift-giving— that will increase my savings over time, enable me to help my son graduate college, and empower me to build that retirement nest egg. This book is "spot on." I'd recommend it for any generation of reader, from late high school on."

—Lisa Berg,
Mother of a College Student

"I've used this book's tips so often that I've done something unprecedented for me: I've bought a second copy, underlined it, and put it in the glove compartment of my car for when "I know there's something I wanted to remember from that book." And I'm not the only one who needs it during our slow economy these days. When I told my men's breakfast group about it, four of the eight members said they wanted a copy (We call ourselves 'The ROMEOs' – Retired Old Men Eating Out!). Finally, Heidi's personal experience with many of the tips has made them seem more do-able, inviting, and it's worth 'giving it a shot.' They have definitely increased my sense of financial control, as she predicts it would in her first chapter."

—Richard Fletcher, Ph.D.

"This book is reinforcing things that were helpful in the former book and raising my awareness yet again of the importance of learning all I can about managing my fixed income. I can especially relate to your point that the answer is not in acquiring more income to solve financial problems, but to spend less and save more. It is making me feel more committed than ever."

—Emily Lanier
Retired School Teacher

"This book is helpful for anyone looking to save because it provides a multitude of examples for different stages of life. Whether you're looking to change your lifestyle or just pick up a few tips, this book is a great source."

—Jonathan Young
Sports Writer

"At last, I'm no longer out of fashion. This book contains myriad good, no-nonsense advice, the kind I was brought up with. I have been applying these recommendations my entire life. This way of life has helped me survive. I heartily recommend this book; it should be part of all young people's education and re-education of older generations.

—Myriam-Rose Kohn
President of www.jedaenterprises.com

"I think your book is complete, practical, and interesting. It contains analysis of the psychological, social, and practical reasons why people avoid saving, why they should save, and lots of good ways they can begin saving now. Trying to follow fashion trends is a trap, along with addiction to impulsive credit card spending. In our growing up years, in the '30s and '40s on the old farmstead, we replaced clothes only when the patches were frayed and the clothes completely worn out! Actually, how a person handles money is a key to their maturity and stability. Bad debts lead to low self-esteem and family conflicts."

—Jerry Swinnerton, M.S.W.

"This book is inspirational and affirming and helps to keep you on the track to wiser money management. I particularly enjoyed the true case studies and got a lot of good information and saving tips from folks in the same situation I find myself. I loved the personal input from Heidi of satisfying that need to buy something new, and if I truly do, the wisest choices for my limited dollars. I learned there is professional help for "over spenders" and organizations I had no idea existed to help curb the urge to spend. A worthwhile read for those grappling with finances."

—Sue Baxter

"This book is a very informative and refreshing addition to TheSmartestWay™ series. After reading the new book, I realized I was straying away from my money-savings goals, as I've been spending on unnecessary wants such as clothes, shoes, and entertainment. It was a good reminder of my spending weakness. This book is a must-read for those who desire to improve on their savings goals."

—Jin Rong
Aerospace Design Engineer

"I was forced to retire from a job I loved at about the same time the economy went sour. I have lost much of my retirement nest egg and have to re-think how I budget my time, money, and resources. Heidi's book has been a rich resource of ideas at just the right time! I have already implemented many of her practical suggestions, including knowing when to shop and who to shop with. As a former shopaholic who could spend hours with friends at the local mall, I have had to rethink my avocation with determined steps to scale down this habit. I now shop outlet stores and thrift stores and look for budget minded sales. Heidi's 10 Question Test in chapter 11 "Save on How to Buy Clothes" is especially helpful. I am learning to walk away from things I only think I need. While I still have a way to go, I know reading and re-reading this practical book will result in a happier and healthier bankbook."

—Betty Ruth Bridgen

OUR MISSION

**To help you spend less so you can save more,
broaden your array of options,
and enrich your life with true value.**

DEDICATION

We dedicate this book to the readers of our first book *TheSmartestWay*™ *to Save, Why You Can't Hang on to Money and What to Do About It.* Many of you told us your personal experiences and how the book helped you. Studies show that stories reach the mind and emotions in a special way, so our favorite parts of our book are your stories about the saving tips you have discovered. This book also is dedicated to all the fans who submitted their essays, including (in order of appearance in the book) Julie Naylor; Isaac Singleton, Jr.; Rebecca Rubin; Emily Lanier; Jonathan Young; Barbara S. Cochran; Steve Staten; Lisa Berg; Jin Rong; Bryan Carey; Myriam-Rose Kohn; Lorie Towsley; and, Richard Fletcher.

On a personal note, speaking of dedication, this book benefited from the tireless care and attention from the highly skilled self-publishing consultant Patt Davis, and we thank her.

We would love to have everyone join our expanding community of sensational savers! Please share with us your personal story, and we will try to include it in our next book, the third in our "three-quel," entitled *TheSmartestWay*™ *to Save Big, The Large Things in Life for Less.* Just email us a brief, approximately 500-word essay to Heidi@TheSmartestWay.

HOW TO READ THIS BOOK

We wrote this book so that you could read it easily in a day. Many readers have told us that they decided to take "just a peek" at one chapter and found they ended up reading the rest of the book in one sitting! On the other hand, you can pick it up briefly and find a solution to a specific situation that can make a difference in your life. The book is designed to be used both ways.

We hope not only that it is enjoyable to read, but also that it helps inspire you to start making a variety of small, easy, and permanent changes that increase your confidence in your ability to save money. They say "the proof is in the pudding," and we know you will see proof in your pocketbook, too. One last favor: Please, after you finish reading and making your notes, pass this book along to others who need it. It is a book that was meant to be shared.

CONTENTS

INTRODUCTION "Why This Book" xvii

Part I: *TheSmartestWay™ to Save –*
IN YOUR HEAD

Chapter 1   Where is Your Head?. 1
Chapter 2   Some Questions to Ask Yourself. 13
Chapter 3   Your Money Style. 21
Chapter 4   Savers' Habits. 29
Chapter 5   Savers' Secrets 43
Chapter 6   Benefits of Saving. 55

Part II: *TheSmartestWay™ to Save –*
ON YOUR DAILY NEEDS

Chapter 7   Saving on Food Shopping. 67
Chapter 8   Saving on Food Handling 79
Chapter 9   Saving on What Clothes to Buy. 89
Chapter 10   Saving on Where to Buy Clothes 99
Chapter 11   Saving on How to Buy Clothes. 111

Part III: *TheSmartestWay™ to Save™ –*
. . . .**ON YOUR "WANTS"**

Chapter 12   Saving on Restaurants 127
Chapter 13   Saving on Other Items. 135
Chapter 14   Saving on Holidays and Gifts 147
Chapter 15   Saving on Parties and Entertainment. 163
Chapter 16   Sam's Principles of Financial
                  Independence – Part II 173

SUGGESTED READING 180

ABOUT THE AUTHORS 190

HOW YOU CAN GET INVOLVED 194

INDEX cciii

INTRODUCTION

WE ALL WANT FINANCIAL FREEDOM. Financial freedom means no more worrying about money. It means you can wake up each morning and know that you have enough money for the rest of your life. The easiest way to increase your personal money supply is: 1. Learn how to save more money, and 2. Learn how to spend less money.

Think about it. It is far easier to save money than to earn it. An added bonus of reduced spending is, unlike increased income, you do not have to pay taxes on your new-found funds! In good times, as well as in not-so-good times, a cash cushion softens unexpected emergencies. A healthy savings buffer is never a bad idea, in either good times or bad. Don't be caught unprepared by the loss of your job, your marriage, or your health. Remember the saying, "The future is not what it used to be." Just because you currently have your health, a job, or a secure marriage does not mean you always will. The same could be said for anticipated inheritances and government entitlement payments. All you can count on is today. A "rainy day fund" is not only a sound financial strategy; it allows for more choices and experiences.

To have financial freedom, you also must learn to live below your income, no matter what it is. Increased income isn't always the solution. For example, if you always manage to outspend what you earn, earning more will not solve the problem, will it? The problem of overspending and shopping addiction is more prevalent than ever in our society. The "b" word (budget) is shunned. Even though the government can print money, the rest of us have limits on what we can spend.

We started writing our first book, *TheSmartestWay™ to Save, Why You Can't Hang on to Money and What to Do About It,* in 2006. We wanted to inspire readers' confidence to hang on to their money. Usually, they said either,

"My [wife/girlfriend/husband/boyfriend] would love it if I read this book!" or "I wish my [wife/girlfriend/husband/boyfriend] would read this book!" At that time, consumers had a negative attitude about saving and a negative savings rate. They not only spent every dollar they earned, they also abused their credit cards and tapped into savings accounts. However, after the stock market crash of 2008, frugality became fashionable. These days, saving is still in style, and for good reason. Frugality is about having more options.

Therefore, we are already writing the third book in our series. It is titled **TheSmartestWay™ to Save Big, The Large Things in Life for Less.** In it, you will find ways to save on very costly topics that are not included in this book, such as, cars, homes, college, weddings, and travel, as well as utilities, legal fees, pets, insurance, and decorating. Also, we will explore shopping addiction, debt, budgeting, banking, credit, bartering, scams, family issues, and making extra money. All three of our books on saving are specifically about saving, not about investing. Saving is the first step to having the resources with which to invest.

Frugality does not mean deprivation. We both were raised to be frugal, but we believe in a life well lived. Sam is the expert, so Heidi learns something new from him every day. One thing we both understand is that changes in behavior have to seem easy or you won't play along. This is not a crash diet, so you will not see overnight results. To continue the food analogy, if it's not on your plate, you won't eat it. If it's not in your wallet, you won't spend it. It is the daily choices, day after day, that drop the pounds and gain the wealth. You and your partner can get on a healthy money diet. You know who the saver is and who the spender is in your relationship. Our books help develop that discussion and, therefore, maintain financial harmony at home.

How to use this book? You can start with any chapter that looks interesting. Just dive in. Make this book the beginning of a "work in progress" for you. You can set up a plan, alone or with a financial partner, to establish some realistic goals and timelines. It may take you a few days, weeks, or even months to read through the book and "make it your own." Just try out the suggestions that sound useful and don't worry about the rest.

Even if tough economic times become more prosperous, you will always benefit from knowing how to save. We hope that the things you read in this book will strike an unguarded segment of your brain and your brain will tell you, "Not only do I need to do it—I *can* do it!"

Life is not just about pursuit and disposal of income. In your life journey, we want you to have mastery over your money, spend less so you can save more, and broaden your array of options to enrich your life with true value.

TheSmartestWay™
TO SAVE —
IN YOUR HEAD

Chapter I

WHERE IS YOUR HEAD?

*"A prudent man foresees the difficulties ahead
and prepares for them;
the simpleton goes blindly on and suffers the consequences."*
—Proverbs 22:3

EVEN WHEN RECESSIONS are declared statistically "over" by economists, that doesn't mean everyone is able to go back to business as usual, buying and spending for today with no thought of saving for tomorrow. We believe that being thrifty will be a permanent, long-term condition among Americans, even when the economy revives. As you learn to live in what is sometimes called "The New Normal," you may recognize some of the following adjustments in your thinking about your finances:

Are you feeling "frugal?"

The cost of living and everything connected with it continues to increase. The single most successful way of coping on a fixed income is to wring more value out of your dollars. You may have heard of people who live better than those who make more than they do. What is their secret? It's all in their head. Frugality is a state of mind and a way of life.

There are many reasons why saving has become an admired and respected trait. Setting aside funds for investment, retirement, emergencies, and charitable goals seems smarter than ever. They've eliminated debt and stress from their lives. People respect savers and ask for their advice and guidance. They're often the ones chosen to become community leaders and business or personal partners. They can manage their family affairs successfully.

People are starting to notice small, recurring expenses and add up what they cost in their totality. People have discovered that they aren't "too proud" to shop at discount stores. Dollar stores and discount stores sales have started booming. Upscale retailers are into the frugality spirit, too. Grocery stores such as Whole Foods offer coupons and weekly sales, Starbucks dropped its price on a cup of coffee, and old-fashioned, classic toys like Legos and Etch A Sketch are making a comeback. Nevertheless, there is one indulgence that appears to be recession-proof and that is chocolate. Whew! After all, the extra antioxidants make it a bargain, right?

Are you feeling hung over from a decades-long shopping binge?

Shopaholic is a cute term. However, real shopaholics have real problems. Do you go on shopping binges, chronically and repetitively shop, and buy things for short-term satisfaction? As you have undoubtedly experienced, the short-term satisfaction can lead to long-term damage to yourself and others. Shopping binges usually result in a hangover of economic nausea, relationship headaches, and buyer's remorse.

How did Americans become addicted to shopping? They got confused about what true value is. Calculating true value can be difficult. We should only buy things that hold perceived value or meaning for us. What is the value and the meaning behind our purchases? Is the value of the purchase an experiential value that you share with someone else, such as a vacation? Does the value of a purchase lie in boosting self-esteem, such as a new suit? Is the value of a purchase a sentimental value, such as jewelry? Shopaholics have to ask themselves hard questions, such as, How can I enjoy new experiences without paying for expensive vacations? How can I boost my self-esteem without buying a new suit? How can I create sentimental memories without buying jewelry?

The answers to these questions can sooth the nausea and pounding temples that result from overspending. The cure for an evening of binge drinking is not another beer. The cure for a shopping binge is not another shopping bag. Reflection is the cure.

Are you feeling economic stress?

It is no surprise that stress soars when the economy tanks. Even in healthy economic times, when people feel economic stress, they tend to suffer from irritableness, fatigue, and sleeplessness. Stress is an equal opportunity killer. It does not care how much money you have or do not have. It strikes in two ways, seen and unseen. It leads to overeating, overconsumption of alcohol or drugs, and smoking, which are visible. It also leads to depression or suicide, which is irreversible.

Internally, stress wears down the body's organs in a cumulative manner as alcohol and cigarettes do. Stress builds up cortisol in the body, leaving one vulnerable to heart attacks, strokes, panic attacks, depression, and bleeding ulcers. We do not want to stress you out (really!) but a heart attack could cost you dearly, even if you have health insurance to pay for it—which is another stressful topic. Why not attack your spending issues, reduce the stress, and avoid the heart attack instead?

Do your best to avoid stress. You can manage stress physically by taking care of your body. Avoid unnecessary drugs, overeating, and overindulging. Feed your body more healthy food, give it more sleep, and make it perform more exercise. You can manage stress mentally and emotionally with meditation, prayer, and yoga and by enjoying various physical activities, hobbies, and friends. As the father of stress research, Hans Selye, once wrote, "It's not stress that kills us; it is our reaction to it."

Here is an added bonus to getting a grip on your reaction to your economic situation. You will spend less money on curing medical and psychological ailments. In addition, you will enjoy your life more!

Are you feeling the Baby Boom busting open?

The massive Baby Boom generation consists of all those born in America between 1946 and 1964. Now they are in their "nesting years." They are building their retirement nest egg. But the recent economic downturn messed with the nest. Retirement accounts were cut in half, pension plans disappeared, and layoffs increased. Would-be retirees are working longer, spending less, and re-envisioning their retirement dreams. Proactive and visionary planning and saving is the way out of the mess.

Baby Boomers were expected to receive an estimated $41 trillion dollars in "generational wealth transfer" inheritance from their elders. However, a recent AARP study says that fewer are now expecting such a windfall and more are expecting less. The main reasons are inflation, taxes, and health care costs. The elderly are living longer than ever and incurring more health care costs than ever. Thirty percent of 65-year-old women and 20 percent of 65-year-old men are expected to live to age 95.

It's best to live your life without hoping for or expecting something that is not guaranteed. The best, but hardest, way to know what to expect in terms of an inheritance is to talk about it. Have that difficult discussion about financial preparation with someone close to you. Then have the discussion with trustworthy financial advisors, such as an attorney, accountant, or financial planner, to make the necessary arrangements and reduce tax exposure. Also, if you receive an inheritance, be watchful against emotional spending. Save and invest your inheritance.

On the other hand, adult children have a responsibility to discuss finances with their elderly parents if they have concerns about how their parents are handling their money. Signs of lack of mental capacity, such as Alzheimer's disease or other dementia set on by advancing age, often are initially very slight.

Are you feeling the squeeze?

More people nearing retirement, the "near elderly" aged 55-64, are figuring out that their later years are going to be longer and more expensive than they had planned. Boomers are becoming eligible for government benefits. In 2010, an estimated 47 million people were enrolled in Medicare, up 38 percent from 1990. By 2030, the number is projected to be a whopping 80 million people!

Unfortunately, the Social Security fund is running low because more retirees are drawing from the fund than workers are donating to it. Scary estimates say that a third of middle-income workers may run out of money after just 20 years of retirement, even with the help of Social Security.

Are you feeling retirement slipping out of reach?

Nest eggs have been raided, pension plans frozen, and retirement incomes are at risk. Fewer pension plans are available. Many boomers have reduced their 401(k) contributions and dipped into their retirement accounts to cover the shortfall from job loss and housing value loss. To make matters worse, when older workers are laid off or lose their jobs, it takes longer for them to find a job than younger workers because they are accustomed to higher salaries. Even if they "played by the rules" and followed the example of their thrifty Depression-era parents, boomers are still pinched by higher health care costs and higher food and fuel costs. They are saving by cutting back on entertainment and non-necessities.

Therefore, for many, "golden" retirement years filled with golf and fishing are being postponed. Boomers are retooling their training and education, recreating themselves, and continuing to work as long as possible. They are earning and saving as much as they are able, as long as they are able. Hopefully, they will find renewed fulfillment in their reinvented lives.

Are you feeling concerned for the younger generation?

Studies indicate that the 50 million young adults in our country tend to be more optimistic about the economy than their parents. They are confident, upbeat, civic-minded, and open to change. A Pew Research Center study says that the Millennial Generation Y (currently teens and twenty-somethings) will also be the most educated generation in American history.

Unfortunately, nearly one third of people in their 20s and 30s require financial support from their family and friends. The high cost of college and unpaid student loans are partly to blame. While older Americans have been trimming their credit card debt, students have been borrowing more than ever. Amazingly, total student loan debt now exceeds credit card debt, with more than $850 billion outstanding. Students need to weigh their loans carefully and learn how to handle their money.

Are you feeling concerned about young people's spending habits?

Parents must keep an eye on their children's shopping habits. Don't just drop the kids off at the mall to entertain themselves with their friends. Malls are not a safe place for them economically or socially. Neither is the media a safe place, because it's difficult to control what your children watch on television and their electronic devices. However, just as you should care about what your children are putting into their bodies, you should care about what they are putting into their minds. Children don't need a television in their bedroom. Families can watch television together and choose programming that meets the approval of the parents.

Don't tune into programs that glorify excessive shopping and extravagant spending. Don't subscribe to catalogs and shopping-oriented magazines. Teach your children that they are so much more than what they own or what they wear. As a result of your concern and vigilance, your child will have happier, more grounded personalities. As an added benefit, they will perform better in school and handle their money better in life.

An esteemed psychologist has issued a warning against girls and young women watching "haul videos." A haul video is an Internet-posted video of a shopping spree. The "vlogger" (video blogger) reports every detail of her endless shopping sprees. Sounds harmless? Apparently not. "The most popular hauls have been viewed by staggering numbers of people, even into the millions," reports shopping addiction specialist April Benson, Ph.D. "Some vloggers are getting addicted to making these videos. At least one 16-year-old is currently being home schooled to allow her more time to haul more stuff, and the seven-year-old sister of another vlogger is taking an early lead in mesmerizing second-grade fashionistas. Retailers are enabling the most popular vloggers by sending them merchandise to review or giving them gift cards as compensation for showcasing their products."

You may think a child's shopaholism and "haul videos" are cute. But you would change your mind if you found out your daughter had become compulsively unable to stop spending your money. Dr. Benson fears that, "Both the makers and the watchers of haul videos are buying into the dark, destructive and deeply false message these videos embody: that whoever said money can't buy happiness just didn't know where to shop." In her book To Buy or Not to Buy: Why We Overshop and How to Stop, she tells how to demagnetize the pull to shop. The pull comes from six powerful magnets: malls and stand-alone stores, internet shopping, television commercials, television shopping channels, catalogs, and magazines. Analyze how much these magnets pull you and your children off-balance into self-destructive behavior and then create a plan to systematically minimize their power.

Are you wondering about the lack of consumer financial literacy?

Consumer financial literacy starts at home. How to handle money can be taught by example from an early age. Unfortunately, many families don't talk about money, they just spend it. However, the world can be a harsh teacher.

If the thought of "saving for retirement" sounds like a monumental goal, start small like saving for a new (or used) sofa or car, then move on to funding a savings account with six-months worth of living expenses for "just in case." Start small and start today to set the steps that you will follow next week and next month. And tell your family, so they will support your efforts and help keep you accountable.

Children desperately need to learn consumer financial literacy not only at home, but also at school, K-12. However, curriculum adjustments are maddeningly slow and teachers acknowledge they are unprepared. Young adults (and 21 is still very young) need to be warned that credit cards are only for real emergencies. They need to be urged to avoid carrying a balance if they have a credit card. They need to understand that the choices they make today will affect the rest of their lives. They need to cherish their now-golden credit rating as the precious key to achieving their financial dreams.

Some young people take advantage of sound financial advice. However, if they don't want to learn money management from their parents, their parents should find a mentor for them. Urge young people to ask their mentor, "What was the best thing you ever did financially? What was the worst financial decision you ever made?"

Young people say they are willing to accept less. They prize the virtues of simple living and autonomy. They switch jobs out of boredom, lack of loyalty, or trying to get ahead. Yet young people can have difficulty finding jobs. Despite their high level of education, their unemployment rate remains much higher than the national rate. Reports say that they may be the first generation in our nation's history to not end up better off financially than their parents.

Make sure you present a positive, realistic role model for your children. They are watching you. Instruct your children on the difference between appearing affluent and being actually wealthy. Surely you've known people who try to appear affluent when they are nearly broke. On the other hand, have you ever noticed how some truly wealthy people sometimes do not appear to be wealthy? Despite outward appearances, a person's bank account is the most accurate sign of true financial wealth. Consumer financial literacy is about learning—and teaching— these concepts.

REAL LIFE CASE STUDY
"Savings Tips from a Savvy Student"
Written by *TheSmartestWay*™ fan Julie Naylor

College is super expensive, so there are a few things to start doing early. When your child is in high school starting freshman year, have them go on www.fastweb.com, or a similar reputable site. Such sites are free and give you information about applying for scholarships. If the child is able to build up at least a few scholarships over time, that'll be extremely helpful. If there's a site where you have to pay to apply, chances are it's a scam.

Ignore all of those grant websites that charge you a fee. If you apply for a grant, make sure it's through a reputable site. Make sure a student fills out the Free Application for Federal Student Aid (FAFSA) early. The earlier they fill it out, the more access to financial aid they'll have.

I had some textbooks from last semester and a software package that was unopened and never used. In this case, I had items I couldn't use, but were worth something. I sold them on www.amazon.com and got more money for them than textbook buybacks. In a case like this, selling online was worth it; if you decide to sell such items, make sure you send them via Media Mail through the USPS as otherwise shipping gets too expensive. (Can you tell I'm an Amazon fan?)

NEVER buy your textbooks at the school bookstore. Always buy online. I paid a fraction of what my peers paid on all of my textbooks last semester because I bought online. My only recommendation would be to email the teacher two weeks before school starts to ensure you get your books in time.

When shopping for groceries, hit the cheapest store first. For example, where I shop, there's a 99 cents store next door to a Whole Foods and a CVS. If I have to get groceries, I go to the 99 cents store first. Usually, I can find a good chunk of my food for the week there, plus any toiletries. Next is CVS for any cosmetics and other toiletries. Then I go to Whole Foods and get the rest of my groceries there. By going to the cheaper places first, I only spend more money on the things I need to spend more money on.

I don't have the money for a gym membership, so I use workout DVDs. You can check these out from your local library or can get them for fairly cheap on www.amazon.com or www.eBay.com. I love this method of working out because you do it from the comfort of your own home, can rotate a few videos to keep things interesting, and don't have to incur the time and expense of commuting. I really like checking the DVDs out on Amazon first, because people will rate them; if I buy one,

I only buy the highest-rated DVD and read the comments so I can have a good idea of what I'll get. I've also found good DVDs for cheap at Ross. For fun and exercise, I recommend hiking and bird watching. These are fun hobbies that hardly cost a thing and can be done almost anywhere!

Chapter 2

SOME QUESTIONS TO ASK YOURSELF

"A wise man thinks ahead;
a fool doesn't, and even brags about it!"
—Proverbs 13:19

PEOPLE NEED to take responsibility for their finances. They need to use their money and not let their money use them. Do you know what your monthly expenses are? Do you have a budget? Do you talk to your family or significant other about your finances? Do you have financial priorities? Do you realize you need to spend less and save more?

Are you worried you might be a debtaholic?

Some people are born with either a "tight fist" or a "hole in the pocket" when it comes to money. Much of our saving and spending inclinations come from our upbringing, our environment, and our peers, as well as our inborn nature. Whether nature or nurture make you what you are, fess up to it and work with it. You and your financial partner can divide the money-handling tasks and get the job done. One of you is better at buying less at the grocery store. One of you is better at balancing the checkbook and paying bills. If you do not have a financial partner, team up with a friend who handles money well.

It is far better to become a super-saver who enjoys life instead of a "big spender" who suffers financial stress. Super-savers are sometimes considered to be "cheapskates" who do not know how to have fun with their money. They could be diagnosed with S.A.D., Spending Anxiety Disorder! Nevertheless, a life of spending wisely does not have to be miserable. Super-savers just do not want to be constantly distracted with consumption and debt. Their solution: spend less than they earn. The result can be less stuff and more contentment.

Do you get close to paying everything off and then finding you are back in the hole again? What is it that drives you away from reaching your financial goals and forces you to be a bondsman to debt? The easiest way to determine whether you're addicted to debt or not is if you find yourself thinking that you need to spend for a financed experience (such as a vacation), goods, or services. Many tell themselves that they "need" something that requires going into debt or taking money earmarked to pay down debt.

The most irrational situation is when someone who wants to escape from debt takes on more debt to help "cope" with debt. One example is to go into debt by taking an expensive vacation to "de-stress" from a stressful job. They return even more stressed out due to the cost of their vacation! To add insult to injury, the stress can lead to overeating and health problems. Reducing the debt instead of adding to it would have been a better solution.

All addictions have similarities. One sign of addiction is denial of the problem until it becomes so uncomfortable or so obvious that it can no longer be denied. Strained relationships, stress, and eventually health problems are often due to financial stress. Everyone has a different "hit bottom" point. If the problem with addictive behavior is not identified and treated before the bottom is hit, the long crawl back from the bottom must begin. It's sad, but "shopaholics," otherwise known as "debtaholics," are currently coddled and celebrated in our consumer-driven society. Addiction, however, is serious and can get out of control and damage lives, sometimes permanently.

An addiction problem can be dealt with honestly and bravely, sometimes alone, but more often with the support of a friend, therapist, and/or recovery group. Debtors Anonymous and other addiction recovery groups are available to help. If you need help, get it.

Are you wondering about overcoming debt addiction?

Everyone has their weakness. For some, it is cooking gadgets, power tools, or shoes. For many, the temptation seems to be expensive electronics. Are you like "a kid in a candy store" when the latest video game, smart phone, or Apple product is released to the market? Ask yourself honestly if the latest electronic gadget brings you lasting happiness. Why not wait until the "early adopters" work out the bugs? Why not wait until the prices drop, which they inevitably will? Then you could stick with your savings plan and still have some fun with your digital toys, too.

Some people are addicted to spending, no matter what they are spending for. The structure of the global auction house eBay has a built-in "desire thermostat" that keeps heating up until the final moments of bidding. That is the good news and the bad news. It is good when you buy something you really need at a good price. It is not good when you find yourself overpaying because "in the heat of battle," you have become committed to conquering the other bidders and become the final victor—at any price.

Another place that people get into problems with spending is in putting too much initial investment into a new business, gambling that it will succeed. In any economy, especially a struggling economy, roll only profits back into a new venture.

You cannot blame others for spending addiction. You must

accept that the choices are yours and your debt-financed lifestyle was a bad choice. To be free from the addiction, you must focus on new goals and values. Move away from pursuing consumption satisfaction to building on sound values. Take pleasure from growing your saving account, instead of depleting it.

If you fear you have an addiction to spending, remove the spending triggers in your life, such as the trips to the mall, the catalogs, magazines, and online "window" shopping. These are high-risk locations for an addict. You need to get truly healed before you are strong enough to allow yourself to be exposed to temptation.

You need to overcome your own deceptions and face up to what you have been doing. Lay out in detail a plan for your life for both the short term and the long term. Look for ways to recognize value and things that bring you to your financial goal.

Do you wilt in "the heat of battle?"

Heidi has friends who like to eat at expensive restaurants and shop at expensive stores. She learned to adapt by ordering something inexpensive, such as soup or a salad. She found there is nothing wrong with going into a store and not buying anything. She could enjoy helping her friends find something they wanted to buy instead. Also, she reads local tourist magazines to discover unusual restaurants and shops that are high in creativity and low on price. Be the creative one in your group who figures out how to have lots of fun without having to use lots of funds.

The funny thing about clothes and cars is that they are the perfect way to appear affluent. We want to encourage you to be more concerned about saving your money and becoming truly wealthy, rather than trying to convince others that you are rich when you're not. On this topic, Heidi has a struggle with herself. Sometimes she finds it too hard to resist telling where she bought something and how little she paid for it, such as when her handbags are considered from Chanel or

Coach or when the hostess at a party walks across the room to say, "I love your dress, where did you get it?" Should you tell your secret? It's hard not to. So, if you start enjoying shopping well and shopping smart, you will start having this enjoyable "problem" too.

Are you ready to take the first step?

The first step in overcoming debt addiction is the same as the first step in overcoming any addiction. You must first admit both to yourself and someone else that you are powerless to overcome your habit without help. Without this admission and coming face to face with the fact that you have an addiction, you are limited in your ability to make sound, unemotional financial decisions.

The second step is to write down a practical plan to manage your addiction. Managing addiction is not easy, but the result is well worth the effort. A complete change in personal attitudes and values is necessary. Your ability to clearly think through wants versus needs, which was discussed in our first book, is essential. Humans are hardwired for desire for the sake of physical survival. Beyond that, if we want too much, we risk being perpetually disappointed, not to mention being perpetually out of money.

Next, you must realize there is no quick fix that will cure an addiction. Quick fixes are only temporary and will end up making the problem worse. With addiction, there is a cycle of feelings. The euphoria of acquiring new things leads to a sense of dismay as it wears off. This dismay and discouragement propels you into the arms of your next quick fix.

Overcome your own deceptions and face up to what you have been doing. Henry Ward Beecher said, "He is rich or poor according to what he is, not according to what he has."

REAL LIFE CASE STUDY

"How to Survive Los Angeles"
Written by *TheSmartestWay™* fan Isaac Singleton, Jr.

In my profession, it is easy to start living above your means. As an actor and voice-over artist, you never know when or what is going to happen next. I have watched other actors who were making about the same income as I was. They went out and bought cars and condos. But you can't assume the money is going to keep coming at the same pace forever. If the income stops flowing, it's a struggle.

Our culture teaches people they need to consume. Los Angeles makes you feel you've got to have a great condo and the latest car. It's as if your material possessions make you who you are. It's the keeping up with the Joneses thing, trying to be something you're not. That is not how I choose to live.

My solution is to start every year knowing that I have enough to pay all my bills for the entire year. Then I just limit myself to that amount. As income comes in during the year, I put a certain amount of that toward building my business. You have to live on what you have and build on it.

There are lots of ways to be smart with your money. I go to Costco for good quality food in bulk. I watch for the lowest gas prices. Usually, I buy my gas at Costco. I ride my bike or walk in my neighborhood. You don't need to eat at a restaurant several times a week. You can cook at home. You don't need to park your car with the valet. You can park yourself and walk a few yards. Some people buy clothes almost every week—but then don't even wear the clothes!

I have only two credit cards, one for personal and one for business. Every month, I pay one off entirely and the other one almost entirely. If you spend cash, you know it is gone. If you use credit cards, you don't realize you are spending money. If you carry a balance on your credit card, you are paying interest. If you pay the minimum payment month after month, eventually *you end up paying for those dinners many times over. Why not save your money, rather than live month-to-month? Do you have to lease an expensive car? You should start with a less expensive car and save your money so you can afford to actually buy—not lease—a better car!*

I learned to save when I was growing up by watching my father and mother. We were upper-middle class and my father was an officer in the Air Force. But my parents taught us that we had to earn our own money for things we wanted. I was going out and mowing lawns when I was 13 years old.

When I was a stunt actor at Disney World in Florida, I knew that I wanted to live in Los Angeles. But I also knew that I shouldn't move to L.A. until I had the wherewithal to survive in Los Angeles. It is much more expensive to live there than in most other cities. So I saved and I planned. By the time I moved out there, I had enough money saved to live without a job for a year and a half. And when I moved there, I already had a job as a stunt actor in the Wild, Wild West and the Water World shows at Universal Studios.

My motto is simple. If you can't afford it, don't buy it. People these days have forgotten that simple rule. That may have been one of the reasons for the housing market crash. God gives us a lot of blessings, but we should make sure we can take care of ourselves. I believe in saving and in planning. It has always worked for me.

Chapter 3

YOUR MONEY STYLE

*"There are people who have money
and people who are rich."*

—Coco Chanel

HERE IS AN EASY WAY to learn about yourself and your money style to help you manage your money. Take this quick quiz and grade it yourself.

Your Money Style

STEP 1:
For each question, circle the letter that best describe you.

1. What is your saving style? Do you:
    a. save a lot?
    b. save only for necessities?

2. What is your reputation about money? Are you:
    a. considered "tight" or "miserly" with your money?
    b. considered very generous and spend without keeping track?

3. What is your shopping style? Do you:
   a. plan your shopping trips carefully with a list?
   b. go on shopping sprees when you feel in the mood?

4. What is your debt level? Are you:
   a. almost entirely free of debt?
   b. in a lot of debt?

5. What is your gifting style? Do you:
   a. spend on gifts carefully?
   b. enjoy giving lavish gifts that you can barely afford?

6. What is your "delayed gratification tolerance?" Are you:
   a. willing to wait for what you want?
   b. the kind of person who thinks, "I want it now?"

7. What is your tax planning process? Do you:
   a. set money aside for taxes and estimated taxes?
   b. wait until your taxes are due and try to find a way to pay?

8. What is your approach to emergency funding? Are you:
   a. saving for a rainy day?
   b. borrowing when emergencies arise?

9. What is your planning for your basic expenses? Do you:
   a. have enough money for what you need?
   b. barely cover your expenses some months?

10. What is your income-to-expenses ratio? Are you:
    a. spending less than you earn?
    b. spending more than you earn?

11. What is your emotional relationship to spending money? Do you:
    a. spend money when you are happy?
    b. spend money when you are lonely, sad, bored, or angry?

12. What is your attitude about your emergency fund? Do you:
    a. regularly put money in your emergency fund?
    b. not have an emergency fund?

13. What is your credit card use? Do you:
    a. rarely use credit card; prefer cash?
    b. often use credit cards or debit cards because they are so much easier?

14. What is your attitude about your debts? Are you:
    a. staying debt free?
    b. having a debt balance every month?

15. What is your level of anxiety about money? Do you:
    a. have peace of mind about money?
    b. have anxiety about money?

16. What are your issues about money and relationships? Are you:
    a. free from money arguments with your loved ones?
    b. arguing about money with your loved ones?

17. How does money lift your spirits? Do you:
    a. feel that saving money lifts your spirits?
    b. feel that spending money lifts your spirits?

18. How often do you borrow money from other people? Are you:
    a. refraining from borrowing money from others?
    b. willing to borrow money if you really want something?

19. How do you handle your checkbook? Do you:
    a. pride yourself in never bouncing checks?
    b. bounce checks occasionally, but it happens to everyone?

20. What is your attitude about windfalls of unexpected funds? Do you:
    a. save or invest money that you receive unexpectedly?
    b. spend money that you receive unexpectedly?

STEP 2:

Add up your a's and b's. If you have 18 or more a's, you have a Saver Money Style (or you at least know what a Saver would do). If you have 15 a's, you have average control of your spending habits. If you have less than 15 a's, you need to work on your spending habits. If you do all 20 in this quiz, write us and tell us how you do it, and we may put you in our next book!

STEP 3:

Now you have a clearer picture of whether you are a Saver or a Spender. How do you feel about it? Write down two goals that will help increase your savings. Make goals that follow the "smart" format: specific, measurable, attainable, and time-related.

Here are some examples of "smart" savings goals:

I will start saving a specific percentage of my money every month until I have saved x amount of money.

I will start keeping a list of everything I buy during the next 30 days.

I will shop only when necessary. I will quit going on spending binges.

I will pay my bills before they are due every month, starting this month.

I will never pay late fees again.

STEP 4:

Now that you have a "smart" goal, write down some "smart" steps to achieve those goals. "Smart" stands for specific, measurable, attainable, and time-related.

Here are some examples of "smart" steps
to achieve your savings goals:

I will take my lunch or coffee to work and put the money that I save on restaurants and coffee stores in my savings account.

I will have a six-month or a year savings cushion.

I will talk to my bank about a better way to handle my banking fees this week.

I will talk with a friend who is a careful spender and learn his or her techniques saving money.

I will put on my calendar a non-negotiable "Pay Bills" appointment with myself each month and pay my bills early, and always avoid late fees.

Keep building your list of "smart" savings goals and "smart" steps to achieve your savings goals!

REAL LIFE CASE STUDY
"Cutting Back on a Medical School Budget -
Part One"
Written by *TheSmartestWay*™ fan Rebecca Rubin
(for more from Rebecca, see the end
of Chapter 6 and the back of the book)

- *While my husband was going through medical school, we learned that we could still enjoy life on a budget. For example, we went out to eat at a restaurant once every week. We found restaurants that offer a good value, comparable to the price of a high quality meal we'd cook for ourselves at home. We researched restaurants on www.dailycandy. com, www.citysearch.com, and www.yelp.com. Another way to save money instead of going out to eat, but still having an amazing meal, is to go out to brunch over the weekend rather than dinner.*

- *If we wanted to go to very nice restaurants, we would have a drink and a small amount to eat before we go out so we weren't too hungry. We would split an appetizer and a main entree, or we each have a salad and split the main entree, and skip dessert.*

- *We tried to avoid events that involved drinking. Alcohol is expensive and potentially dangerous in a city where the infrastructure is centered on driving. I often met friends for free lectures at universities, gallery openings, or readings, and we would have coffee afterward, or hang out at friends' homes. I would meet friends to go hiking or for a walk on the beach. We never gambled or played poker. We went to free jazz or music concerts.*

- *If we are going out for dinner with another couple, we often would tell the hostess or waitress to place the order on separate checks before we sit down to eat. This prevented us from having to split the check 50/50 with a people who ordered much more than we did.*

- *We would go out for coffee or iced tea if we were out for the day running errands, etc. But only occasionally; it is not an everyday ritual. We would buy a song on iTunes for 99 cents instead of three new albums. I would get a manicure once in a while, but not every week.*

- *I read book reviews in the New York Times and L.A. Times, and New Republic. When I heard that one of my favorite authors was coming out with a new book, or there was a book I wanted to read, I called the library as soon as possible and put myself on a waiting list for it, because new releases are often in popular demand. While I was waiting for the book to become available, I often checked out the author's prior books. I'm an avid reader, and the library saved me hundreds, if not thousands of dollars. I also checked out DVDs and books on tape from the library. They send out automatic email notices when a book has arrived or will be due at least four days in advance, and this helped me to avoid overdue charges.*

- *Also, I used www.dailycandy.com as a resource to find out about book swaps. Keil's, the cosmetics line, has a book swap at select stores, and you can bring books you are finished with to trade for new books to read. I do love books, and this does not mean I don't buy books, but I buy books that are essential to a project, or that I will need to use as a reference for a project, or that I feel are essential to own.*

- *When we traveled, I brought snacks and bag lunches. I made sure I packed everything we would need so we wouldn't have to buy replacements while traveling. We shopped online for the most competitive airline price or used our frequent flier miles.*

- *When we went on vacation, we found deals, and we sub-scribed to hotels at our favorite places to find out if they were offering any deals. For example, we recently returned from Two Bunch Palms in Desert Hot Springs and they had an offer to stay two nights, get the third night free.*

- *We have been able to see, experience, and enjoy ourselves a lot while not spending a lot of money. What seems to work is being extremely aware of what we have, what we spend, and how to stay focused on our goals.*

Chapter 4

SAVERS' HABITS

"Money frees you from doing things you dislike.
Since I dislike doing nearly everything, money is handy."

—Groucho Marx

A S WE SAID in our first book, one of the explanations for people's ability to save depends on their habits. Firmly ingrained habits can increase your ability to postpone the desire for "instant gratification." If you have a low tolerance for delayed gratification, here are some ways to strengthen your "savings muscles. One strategy is to find a way to make saving your money a gratifying endeavor. Another way is to make your goal very specific. Also, you can have a vivid, sensory image of what you will experience as the result of your saving. Here are some easy, no time, no-cost ways to strengthen your good-habit muscles like savers do.

Savers start small

The larger the goal for any personal challenge, the stronger the natural resistance to it. Therefore, try to "sneak up on yourself" by setting small, easy goals first. Tie new good habits to old, established habits. For example, most people brush their teeth twice a day without fail. It is a built-in habit. As we said in our first book, ***TheSmartestWay™ to Save, Why You Can't Hang onto Money and What to Do About It,*** if you want to memorize a positive affirmation about money, post it on your bathroom mirror, read it, and think about it while you're brushing your teeth. It doesn't take any extra time out of your day. It is adding value to your regularly scheduled habits. Another regular habit is locking your seat belt before starting your car. When you hear the "click" of the seat belt, develop the habit of affirming that you are careful with your car and careful with your money.

When you accomplish your small goals, such as saving a small amount each week and putting it into the cookie jar, tell yourself how easy it was, and that you are such a good goal-setter and good goal-keeper. Then start on a list of incrementally more difficult goals. Sam knows a receptionist who was a single mother and had a day job. Her practical plan to start small and build her savings was to get a second job in the evening to pay off her debts. Her teenage children obtained after-school jobs and they set aside a special evening on the weekend to spend together.

Savers start small, but they also splurge small. Splurges are necessary so you don't feel like you are constantly depriving yourself. That once-routine random snack or lunch out will feel like a splurge if it's not a daily occurrence. Splurge, but in a small way, when you reach one of your goals and establish new, money-related habits.

When you start small, you are starting, and that is key. It gets the momentum rolling. Once you finally start, it is easier to keep going. Starting is much easier when you start small, so start small today!

Savers take the first step

Develop a timeline and action steps. Each step builds stronger habits. Do one thing today that will set you toward your savings goals. Here is an example. Plan to go to the bank tomorrow and open a savings account. Make it a friendly account. Give it a name, such as the "Caribbean Cruise Fund" or the "If I Lose My Job Fund."

Organize your life to have enjoyment and fun in no-cost ways, such as hiking, visiting museums, and volunteering. Avoid expensive purchases that have hidden costs. For example, a luxury car will require higher insurance and license fees and possibly use more gasoline than an economy car. The day you drive a new car off the lot, you throw thousands of dollars out the window in lost value, now that it is officially "used" and no longer "new."

So many people have heard about the famous "latte factor." They know that ordering expensive coffee drinks at the corner coffee shop is cutting into their long-term savings goals. But how many people make the decision to drink free coffee at the office or bring their own coffee from home? It seems like a small step, but it can save hundreds of dollars per year. Pack a healthy lunch or snacks instead of buying expensive and unhealthy snacks at vending machines or restaurants. This can save several thousands of dollars per year. Knowing doesn't equal doing. Only doing puts all that extra money into your savings account!

Savers are aware of bad habits

Awareness is the first step. Think of a bad money habit that you want to eliminate. First figure out why you do what you do. What is the payoff? Be honest with yourself. What do you get from this behavior—attention, a thrill, self-esteem? Figure out how to get what you need another way. How badly do you want to get rid of the bad habit? Are you fully convinced, or is someone else telling you what you should do?

When you eliminate the unwanted habit, don't leave an empty space. Fill it with a positive habit. Take control and retrain your brain. Your new replacement habit should be something that is easy and satisfying. For example, replace daily latte at a coffee shop with sitting on a park bench with a healthy snack. Heidi likes to add new positive behaviors to other behaviors that are already good habits. She attaches the new good habits to the old good habits. This technique takes less effort. As we mentioned in our first book, **TheSmartestWay™ to Save, Why You Can't Hang onto Money and What to do About It,** if you want to remember to tell yourself positive money affirmations, post them on your mirror, and read them when you brush your teeth every morning and evening. You will backslide occasionally. Everyone does!

What separates the winners from the losers is that when winners fall down, they get back up again and keep going forward. If you fall off the wagon, get back on it. You can always begin again.

Savers can define bad habits

Yes, we are asking you to consider changing a few behaviors, a few bad habits, one at a time. Choose which ones make sense for you. Choose the easiest one first. It is okay to feel awkward or uncomfortable changing a behavior.

Here is a list of bad financial habits. You may find some that apply to you and some that you recognize in others:

1. Keeping up with the Joneses. This tendency reveals a lack of inner confidence. Do you spend money on things that do not contribute to your personal financial independence in order to gain the false admiration of others?

2. Choosing short-term, immediate gratification. Motivate yourself to think long term by visualizing the success and the happy feelings you experience when you achieve your long-term goals.

3. Using debit and credit cards and other "time savers." Debit cards can cost you money through bank fees and cost you time with hassling with the bank. Convenience now can waste your time later on. There is an old phrase,

"You can choose easy now and hard later, or hard now and easy later." Which do you choose?

4. Failure to look at alternatives. If you comparison shop, you can find items, such as appliances, that perform the same function at substantially lower prices.

5. Failure to negotiate prices. If you don't ask, you don't get, right?

6. Giving gifts in an attempt to buy affection or friendship. Gift giving can be a very expensive habit. Can you cut back and give value to your friends and family in more creative, meaningful ways?

Everyone has acquired at least a few bad financial habits along the way. The solution is to recognize them and figure out how to overcome them.

Savers replace bad habits with good habits

Here is a simple bad habit to break and a simple good habit to take its place. Replace ATM use with planning ahead. ATM use can create bad habits that nibble or even gobble your funds. The use of an ATM can trigger an overdraft and the resulting checking account overdraft fees and checking account chaos. Ready cash through frequent ATM use can result in overspending or spending more than you had intended to spend. Replace your overuse of ATMs with the simple habit of planning your cash. Use cash from an envelope designated for each planned purchase.

Another easy habit is to start ordering less at restaurants. Do not be afraid to appear "cheap." You can order an appetizer as an entrée and split a dessert. You can order the smaller sized entrée salad. You can skip wine or sodas and order tap water. These days, restaurants are just happy to have you walk in the door. If you are tempted to spend when you have plastic in your wallet, try not taking a credit card with you. Some people find that they are less likely to spend if they carry only large bills.

Bad habits are our irrational mind overpowering our rational mind. The self that wants to have a large emergency fund can get strong-armed by the self that wants to sign up for a luxury cruise. The weakness in succumbing to temptation is a battle that continues to be waged in everyone's lives. It is a part of being human. Fortunately, persistence will help you overcome bad habits.

Savers find the flip side of bad habits

Most good habits are the flipside of bad habits. For example, instead of spending money to keep up with others, get into the habit of ignoring what others may think and focusing on your own needs.

1. Instead of spending on wants, spend on needs.
2. Instead of fulfilling impulses, resist impulses and save for long-term financial rewards.
3. Instead of buying without comparing, get into the habit of comparing.

To replace bad habits with good habits, you have to apply creativity. Your mind can overwhelm your ability to be creative when it becomes overwhelmed with worry. Your mind needs to be free from fear in order to think creatively and confidently. If you feel yourself getting burdened by pressured, panicked thoughts that seem to swirl in circles, you need to dial down the spinning so you can actually think. Turn off and tune in. That means, turn off the TV, the computer, the news, and the music. Tune into what is really going on in your head. You may be surprised by what you hear.

What gives you peace of mind? Do you like long walks, meditating, yoga, talking with someone wiser? Prayer and affirmations can help, too. What you focus on is what you get. Just like driving a car, if your eyes turn to the side of the road, your car drifts in that direction, too.

Look around at friends and the people around you. Are they encouraging your own inner positive self-talk? We start to look and act like the people around us. Find stories of people who overcame difficult circumstances. They had to work hard, as you need to do. They had to keep telling themselves they would succeed, as you need to do. Tell yourself, "If they can do it, I can do it, too." Let their lives be a model for how you can make your life better.

You will find yourself living better and feeling better when you start to gain mastery over some of your bad financial habits and replace them with good financial habits. Take a few moments today to think creatively about how to accomplish this.

Savers set goals

Savers know how to set goals and avoid the goal-setting demons. Goal-setting demons are the self-criticizing mindsets that keep you from achieving your goals. Savers, like all achievers, set goals. They set goals that will work for them. Everyone is different. Do not let others tell you what your goals should be. Only you can determine the goal that your inner psyche is willing to fixate on. The one that juices you up and helps you marshal your emotional resources to aim for the target.

That being said, here is the most worthy goal we can recommend to you. In general, everyone needs a cash cushion. How many months of income are up to you. Where is your comfort level? Put that no-touch money somewhere that is out of reach from temptation, yet is also "liquid" enough that you can get your hands on it in an emergency. Speaking of emergencies, how do you define the word emergency in terms of your cash cushion? Your cash cushion should be saved for only real emergencies, the ultimate needs of food and shelter, and nothing else.

A recent survey showed a 50 percent drop in the number of people who make New Year's resolutions. The main reason for this statistic is that people are afraid of failure. They hate to make a resolution, fall short of achieving it, and then feel rotten about it. The typical categories of resolutions are to improve the head (self-improvement), the heart (romance), the waistline (diet), and, perennially, the wallet (finances). Goal setting is good, but sometimes the goals themselves are not quite right. Was your goal too grand and unattainable? If you set your goal too high and you don't attain it, you could become discouraged, which is a setback emotionally.

On the other hand, was your goal one that you are truly committed to? Was it not really your true heart's desire? Was it put in a negative way, like "stop doing" this? Set your goals the right way and you will have much better success.

Savers work their plan

While planning is essential, it is only the first step. Planning without doing won't get you anywhere. You need a road map to where you're going, but then you have to get on the road and move. If your goal looks too large, then "the only way to eat an elephant is one bite at a time." It is doing that that results in getting, because "without doing there is no getting."

Automatic savings plans can launch you toward you savings goals. Your paycheck can be automatically deposited by your employer. This results in saving you time, earning you more interest (since your money goes into your account earlier), and most importantly, putting you on a guaranteed road to financial success. Talk to your employer about it.

As we discussed in our first book, do not spend money on things you do not need. This is not as easy as it sounds. "Is it a want—or is it a need?" is a complicated question. Often, people think of many of their wants as needs. Hard times, however, require hard questions. The answers redefine one's concepts of wants versus needs. For example, does your elementary school child really need a cell phone—with an expensive text messaging package? Does your first baby really need to be driven around in a large SUV? Do your teenagers really need a car? And if they do, can they earn it? You will be surprised by the number of trimmable expenses you can find. Just think of them as "trimmables" that you can cut back now and add later if necessary.

Which would you rather have, a high-fashion wardrobe—or your own home? While many say that they want their own home, they may not have thought through the daily choices that are required to reach that goal. A six- to 24-month change in lifestyle may be all that is necessary, but it requires a dramatic adjustment in one's thinking, attitude, and actions.

Savers visualize the future

One of the most popular techniques for accomplishing goals is the visualization of the process of accomplishment, as well as of the rewards to be gained from reaching your goals. Can you visualize what it will be like when you are debt free? Try and imagine how this will be by writing down all of the positive things that will come from it.

When you visualize the accomplishment of your savings goal, what will be your reward? When you visualize the achievement of your success, employ all of your senses—sight, sound, touch, even taste. Will you be standing on the front step of your new home, watching your hand turn the key to the front door, and hearing the sound of children playing nearby? Will you be sitting in the driver's seat of your new car, inhaling the "new car" scent? Will you be eating lobster at a beach-side café on a remote island, listening to calypso music, and watching a sunset? The process of imaging creates positive triggers that resemble the feelings of actual gratification.

If you have not yet achieved financial independence, visualize how you will feel when you achieve it. Financial independence occurs when the income you receive from investment sources exceed your needs. We're not talking about "wants," but "needs." There are those who will never feel that they have enough income to exceed their wants. But almost all of us can reach that place where our financial means will provide what we need to be happy. The visualization process requires us to be as specific as possible, write out these feelings, and then spend a small part of everyday for visualization of them being accomplished.

Visualization, of course, is not enough by itself. Those mental pictures must be translated into action. They are not a substitute for action, but tools to motivate you into action.

Self-hypnosis is another technique to help you become a better saver. There are seven steps to self hypnosis as outlined in Drs. Don Moine and Ken Lloyd's best-selling book called "Unlimited Selling Power." Drs. Moine and Lloyd point out that repetition is the best way to retain what you are learning. Studies show that with each repetition, your retention will be greater. The more you know about a subject, the better you will be able to master it. You can never know too much about how to handle your finances. An initial reading of a book will result in only 10 percent retention, a second reading may raise that level to 30 percent, and a third reading can bring it up to 50 percent or more.

Read books on financial literacy and how to save money. Take in the information and the advice. Visualize yourself following the suggestions that make sense for your life. With time and practice, you will not only be visualizing, you will actually be doing better with your money.

Savers get organized

Everyone has felt disorganized about their finances at some point in their lives. When that happens, it is time to simplify. Complexity leads to confusion and confusion leads to mistakes. This is no time to make mistakes that cost you money. You want to save your money, not waste it foolishly or unknowingly. Gather up all your receipts and records. Sift through the pile. Sort everything into its own category. Put each topic into its own labeled file folder. If you don't know what to keep and what to shred, just keep the following for a year:

statements from banks, utilities, and credit card companies. Keep forever: insurance policies, receipts for major purchases and renovations, titles, and warranties.

If you share your finances with a spouse, significant other, or family member, do not give up control of what is yours and what is your responsibility. Get your own separate bank account, even if you have a joint account. Yours, mine, and ours makes it easier to keep track of the funds. Talk with your financial partner about your joint goals for your combined assets, and also what you want and need to do with the money in your own account.

Take responsibility for at least knowing how the joint funds are being handled. Co-habitating couples have legal financial rights and obligations to each other, depending on how they co-mingle their funds. Find out what those rights and obligations are in your area. You may co-own assets together, depending on the laws in your area. The legal system sees you as equal.

Savers forego convenience

Many of the "cool" things in modern life promise time-saving convenience. From the invention of the washing machine to the latest iPhone apps, it's all about making life easier, faster, and hassle-free. Set aside for a moment the notion that these conveniences free up "extra time." Take a long look at all the extra costs these conveniences can rack up, and the time that they take to fix any malfunction. Conveniences, which are offered so enticingly to consumers, are often expensive. Many of the new conveniences in our fast-paced lives have hidden additional costs. To plan ahead for purchases is a bit inconvenient, but it soon becomes an easier habit with practice. Think ATM fees, bank fees, investment fees, and credit card and debit card interest (if you overdraw your account).

Savers take a look at their lifestyle and analyze "conveniences" carefully. To save money, you need to make spending less convenient, not more convenient. If you tend to spend whatever cash is in your wallet, limit what you put it there. If you tend to use credit cards too much, carry only one.　Better yet, leave it at home. If you suffer from frequent "emergencies" that require going into debt, why not plan ahead for those situations and create a buffer emergency account?

Savers are willing to forego convenience when it costs more to spend than it costs to save. Actually, saving is cost-free. Spending, however, is more expensive than ever. As we explained in our first book, when you spend a dollar, it costs you at least a $1.60. That's because you pay income taxes on the dollars you earned. And you also, in my circumstances, have to pay a local and state sales tax. Of course, this varies slightly depending on your income tax bracket and where you live. But as of this writing, higher taxes are on the table to address national and state deficits.

Savers take a closer look

Here is a simple project you can start doing today. Look at your credit card statements closely. What are the small, recurring automatic withdrawals for? Which of those items or expenses can you trim back? Automatic billing can be a money-sapper. As soon as the seller has your credit card number and permission to bill you monthly, they own you. Find all the charges that are automatically deducted from your account. Arrange to cancel these items if at all possible.

Automatic deductions might be those magazine subscriptions you do not have time to read or that health club membership you seldom use. Analyze all of your monthly membership dues. If working out at the health club will strengthen you physically and mentally, it is a good investment; you may be saving on extra health care expenses. On the other hand, just because you signed up for a gym membership does not mean you have to keep it forever. Earlier in Sam's career, he conceived and built the premier tennis and horse-riding club in Malibu. He recalls that the managers of the club did everything they could to encourage members to pay with automatic billing. Many people, including celebrities, joined the club, but a noticeable number of members didn't use the facilities often, if at all. Some paid annual membership fees for 10 years or more, even though they used the facility only three or four times. Unless you are someone with unlimited funds and very sure you will use the facility frequently, don't sign up for automatic deduction payments.

Watch out for "free" samples of products or purchases that include a monthly shipment of the product that you "can cancel at any time" in the small print. Heidi has found that it is difficult to convince a company to stop shipping and billing. If you call them and they keep sending the products and the invoices to you, send everything back marked "Return to Sender/Postage Due." Then call your credit card company and insist that they take the charges off your card.

REAL LIFE CASE STUDY
"Frugality as a Family Tradition"
Written by *TheSmartestWay*™ fan Emily Lanier

My family has deep roots in Scotland, so I was probably born frugal. I grew up on a not-too-prosperous farm where nothing went to waste. Table scraps were scraped into the "slop bucket" for the pigs. Things like outer leaves of lettuce and cabbage went to the chickens. These days, I compost table scraps with yard waste to feed the soil.

When I got married, I learned even more about saving from my mother-in-law. She never threw anything away that was edible. She'd take a left over little bit of this and a little bit of that, add them to whatever was cooking with seasonings, and it was always tasty. Scrambled eggs get more interesting with almost any bits of leftover's mixed in, from spinach to meats.

The same goes for pastas—bound with a cream soup if you like. We often had a small bowl each of "wonder salad." You'd wonder what all was in with that lettuce. But it was always delicious, always nutritious.

Later on, I learned to make low-cost, nutritious soups by asking for bones at the meat counter of the grocery store. The butcher often just throws them away, but they are filled with nutrition. I simmer the meat bones for several hours or put them in a crockpot over night with onion, salt, and a few tablespoons of vinegar to draw out the calcium. They make a delicious broth. To this stock, I add a collection of leftover veggies saved in the freezer and leftover meats. If you like a thicker soup, stir in a few tablespoons of flour mixed with cold water, or a few tablespoons of instant grits or cream of wheat. For a creamy soup, thicken with instant mashed potatoes.

As for budgeting for your house and your wardrobe, I do believe in buying a few things new, such as shoes and mattresses. Living in a cold climate requires a warm coat, and I buy one every five to 10 years. I wait until the spring when coats are marked down for quick sale. I recently bought a new fleece jacket originally priced at $70. It was marked down three times, to $23.99! Usually, I buy my clothes at nice thrift stores.

I recently heard some good advice: live not within your means, but below your means. That equates to buy your needs, not your wants. Have a savings buffer for almost a year's worth of expenses. We need to find more enjoyment in saving than in spending. For a spending-oriented society like ours, that's a challenge!

Fortunately, I have always been frugal, and have enjoyed saving money all my life. My amazing thrift store and garage sale deals are a point of pride with me. I have taught my children this, too. It must be all that Scottish blood in our veins! To spend frugally and save wisely has always been a guiding lifestyle principle. I both recommend it and embrace it.

Chapter 5

SAVERS' SECRETS

"Money is in some respects life's fire:
it is a very excellent servant,
but a terrible master."

—P.T. Barnum

O NE OF SAM'S FAVORITE phrases is, "Attitude is more important than aptitude." You may know what you need to do, but you also have to want it. Try to set up exercises that make savings a want rather than just a need. You can enhance your attitude toward savings by using an affirmation or mantra.

A mantra is something that you repeat to yourself continuously when you get up in the morning, when you're about to have a meal, and before you go to bed (at least 15 times a day is a good target). Here's a mantra: "I must earn $1.60 to spend $1.00." Another successful mantra is, "I will get everything I want in the future if I spend only on needs now." Find one or more mantras that fit your personality and that help reinforce a positive attitude towards thrift.

Most urges to buy are impulsive. Take the time to consider and weigh the value of a purchase. If you think about it long enough, the "need" to buy that "want" will go away. Before you go shopping, tell yourself, "I will only buy what is on my shopping list." When you are ready to buy, ask yourself, "Did I plan for this purchase? Do I have the cash right now?" When you find yourself buying things you shouldn't, you can tell yourself, "I CAN make better choices about my spending." You can keep it simple. Tell yourself, "I CAN do this." This self-reminder becomes automatic. Find an affirmation that resonates with your soul and start using it today. Here are some more secrets of savers:

Savers talk nice to themselves

You may be struggling with negative self-talk and not even know it. Is there a little voice inside your head that often gives you negative feedback, such as, "Why didn't you do that better, sooner, faster, etc.?" The little voice may be so soft, and seemingly part of your own thinking, that you don't realize that it is negative self-talk. Don't be your own harshest critic. Instead, let others have the pleasure!

Call out your inner critic, sit it down, and give it a scolding. If you aren't your own best friend, who will be? Examine the negative self-talk messages. Why do you listen to them? They can't possibly help you! Can you revise the messages so that they are more encouraging and beneficial? You should be your own biggest cheerleader! Tell yourself that you are doing a great job, that you are doing the best you can with what you have to work with under the circumstances.

Be your own best friend. Listen to yourself for a few minutes. Do you hear negative self-talk such as, "I'm not good with money," or "I am a shopaholic," or "I just can't control my spending." If you were your best friend, you would sit you down and give you a pep talk. You would say, "I know it's hard, but I believe in you. I believe that if you can start making a few positive changes, you will start to feel better about yourself. You will start to see results if you keep on going. I know you can do it." Be that friend to yourself.

Design your own private money-talk affirmation, such as, "My savings account is growing because I'm making good choices," or "I am gaining abundance and true wealth in my life," or "Every day, I am getting better at saving." The elimination of subtle, self-sabotaging behaviors is a no-cost technique that helps you stay on your spending plan.

Savers put their own oxygen mask on first

You have to save yourself before you can save others. Make sure you have your own savings buffer. "Pay yourself first" to build that buffer. Examine your resources and determine the amount that you can save, usually between 10 to 40 percent of after-tax income.

Generally, the more income you have, the higher the percentage this should be. The percentage of savings will vary depending on the part of the country you live in. Those who live in rural areas may be able to save a greater percentage of their income than those who live in metropolitan areas. The cost of meeting basic needs varies dramatically throughout the country. But there are great opportunities to save in metropolitan areas. For example, you may be able to find a wide variety of thrift stores and pre-owned merchandise, parks, free attractions, and entertainment in the city.

The first act is to put aside the amount you have to pay in taxes, followed by the amount that will go into your savings and investment programs. Everyone is subject to a barrage of advertising and encouragement that we get from our family and closest friends to spend. Very few have the will power and discipline to set aside funds towards financial independence rather than spend for immediate gratification. There are, however, several ways of "paying ourselves first."

Keep in mind that generally, the more income you have, the higher the percentage of savings is possible. The percentage itself is not important, but what is important is the attitude. Put your own oxygen mask on first, and take care of business.

Savers don't make excuses

Excuses are funny things. Sometimes we don't even know we are using them. What are your excuses for not saving? If you are young, your excuse may be that you will have plenty of time to save later. It's easy to overspend and under-save when you're young. When you're older, you may fear that it's too late to save. It's never too late. If you think you don't have time to save, you can change that with an automatic deduction. Hold a family meeting to enlist your family's help. Even if you believe you don't earn enough money to save, you could find a few small areas to cut back that can add up. If your employer offers a retirement plan, you should participate, even if you think you can't afford to. Figure out a way.

Perhaps you are one of the lucky ones who earn so much money that you think you don't need to save. Understand that your earning power will ebb and flow. Economies and circumstances go up and down. Isn't it better to tuck away some of that bounty just in case your income may fluctuate sometime in the future?

There is a little poem, "Two men looked through prison bars. One saw the mud; the other saw the stars." The best attitude for success is not to blame, but to have an "attitude of gratitude." Find an internal sense of control over your life. With self-determination, you can take difficult circumstances and make them into something positive. There is a phrase related to driving a car, "Lean into the curves."

You also can use boat metaphors. A savings reserve is like a life preserver. It also is like a like a boat keel. Boat builders know that the deeper the keel of a boat, the more stable it will be in a storm. Everyone is adjusting to changing circumstances. Learning adaptation is learning mastery. When a challenge comes along, don't blame others or circumstance. Instead, deepen your keel. It's time to stop making excuses for not saving.

Savers take responsibility

You may have to "get tough" with yourself when it comes to saving. One way is to create a powerful time distance between the exposure to a desire to spend and the actual purchase. Require that you take the time necessary to consider whether the expenditure is really one that helps you meet your objectives.

If you have a large income and are unable to save, a business manager or bookkeeper can help balance your budget. Set your goals clearly and make sure they are moving you in the right direction.

The point is, you have to look at your life realistically. No one can do that for you. No one is going to care about your future as much as you do because no one is living your life for you. The choices you make or do not make will affect the rest of your life. Sometimes it is difficult and uncomfortable to take those important steps, but sometimes life is about responsibility.

It is easy to make excuses, but excuses don't make the situation any easier. The key to overcoming excuses is to detect them and call them out. We can only look within. We can't blame others, even if they are at fault. Maybe you were scammed and defrauded, maybe you were deprived of an important opportunity, or maybe you were born into deprived and difficult circumstances. Whatever the situation, you are the only one who can live your life. Take responsibility for where you are in your life and press forward. As John F. Kennedy said, "A man can fail many times, but he isn't a failure until he begins to blame somebody else."

Savers acknowledge the "gender gap"

The fact that you might be a woman is not an excuse for not taking care of business when it comes to money. Traditionally, parents have been more inclined to treat their sons and daughters differently when it comes to teaching them about money. Despite increased awareness, the unconscious stereotypes still persist. The typical reality is that mothers take their daughters shopping for entertainment, while fathers gravitate toward sports events and non-spending activities. Society teaches girls that it is fun to shop and that they need to dress in the current fashion to be acceptable in society. Boys, on the other hand, are taught to develop their self-image by competing in the games of life, in sports when they are young, and in the business world as they grow up. The dynamic can be reduced to the question, were you taught as a child to make money, or to spend it?

Women, often cast in the caregiver role, often seem hesitant to take ownership and control of their finances. This comes from generation upon generation of cultural programming that men handle money well and women don't. Even in our modern society, it is not uncommon for a married woman to have an arrangement with her husband that he handles this area of their lives. On the other hand, some husbands leave the household finances to their thrifty wives. Figure out who is best at saving money and let that person handle it. Then make sure that both parties are fully trained about how to take over the finances, if necessary. Relinquishing control doesn't mean relinquishing responsibility.

Women, please don't wait until an emergency situation occurs, such as death, disability, or divorce, before you ask your financial partner the all-important questions. You know what those questions are. You should both know the location of all your bank accounts and investments and how to access them. Remember, in the blink of an eye, the game board's pieces of life can be rearranged and the tables of responsibility turned upside down.

Savers are careful if they are single women

Single women need to understand that "someday my prince will come" is not a strategy. If you are a woman who is starting to learn about how to save money, ask smart people how to do it. Identify emotional blocks that keep you from saving money. Smart women know that starting small is still a start. If they haven't started saving yet, they need to start saving today!

Ninety percent of women in this country will be responsible for managing their finances at some point in their lives. Studies show that many women have substantially less money to live on than men in their later years due to a number of factors. Statistically, women live longer than men. The average age of widowhood is age 56. In the case of a wife surviving her deceased husband, which happens frequently, she needs to know how to handle the household finances, especially if she has children depending on her. Similarly, women need to know how to handle their finances in the case of a divorce.

Women are on par with men in retirement planning. But last year, they became less likely than men to pay their credit card balance in full each month and have an emergency savings fund, according to a study by education firm Financial Finesse.

Savers act like billionaires

Some billionaires are proud of their frugality. For example, Warren Buffet is reputed to still live in the home he bought in 1957 for $31,500. Some billionaires avoid spending on luxury items. Buffet has said, "Most toys are just a pain in the neck." Some billionaires take public transit and shop at average-priced clothing stores. For example, some Silicon Valley gurus ride their bikes to work and wear jeans and t-shirts. Some billionaires buy a dependable car and drive it as long as it will run. IKEA founder Ingvar Kamprad drives a 10-year-old Volvo. Just because they have money and could afford to spend lavishly, some don't. They earmark their funds for more effective and meaningful uses.

Billionaires do not feel pressure to appear wealthy. The people around them already know that they are rich. They tend to be a bit more immune to peer pressure and focus instead on what they really need in order to be satisfied with their own lives. Be like a billionaire in your own self-image. Know that you know how to live well on your own terms.

You don't need to prove anything to others. You just need to prove to yourself that you are using your money in the most effective and meaningful way which meets your own needs and wants. If you worry about what other people think, face the harsh reality that people are not as focused on you to the degree that you think they are. Instead they, like you, are busy worrying about what others are thinking of them!

The most important words that you must be able to admit freely, openly, and often are, "I can't afford it." You must learn to ignore your friends and your own mental urgings when you're tempted to buy something that will move you into debt or away from paying down debt. The bottom line is to value relationships and financial independence over material things. This is the only way to have a stress-free, happy, and content life, whether you are considered wealthy or of more modest means.

Savers understand it is just a matter of more zeros

It may be difficult to change your habits and learn to save, regardless of your income level. "It would not be hard to save if I had a lot of money," you may argue. Nevertheless, a high net worth does not guarantee an ability or understanding of how to save and spend wisely. Wealthy people may even have more trouble keeping track of their money than those with average incomes. Their money is plentiful, spread out over different investments, and they may not have been raised with examples from their family about how to conserve their funds.

People who consider themselves to be wealthy need to look at where their wealth is coming from. Do they have a high-net worth (possessing non-income-producing assets such as homes, cars, collectibles, etc.)? Or do they have high income flow (large amounts of income from steady income streams)? If their net worth comes from assets, how "liquid" are those assets? In other words, could the assets be sold quickly if a large amount of cash was needed due to unplanned circumstances?

People tragically have invested their entire net worth in Ponzi, and now "Madoff," schemes. Their mistake was to put all of their assets into one investment. Even investors worth more than a billion dollars have been tricked this way. Wealth does not protect you from being scammed. It actually makes you a target. The same goes for the ability to save what you need to save. Savers save even if they have a high net worth. They know that their wealth does not protect them from the need to do so.

It is not difficult to spend all of your paycheck, even if you add more zeroes at the end of amount on the check. With just a bit of effort, most folks could find something they wanted to buy if they had an extra hundred dollars or thousand dollars "burning a hole" in their wallet. Such is the frailty of human nature. As mentioned in our first book, **TheSmartestWay™ to Save, Why You Can't Hang onto Money and What to Do About It,** one of Sam's clients had an income of several million dollars a year and yet had nothing in the way of assets to show for it. Why? She spent all of the money she received and more every year. Therefore, she was going deeper in debt every year on a multimillion dollar income that was far in excess of her real needs.

REAL LIFE CASE STUDY

"Eating Well on Less"

Written by *TheSmartestWay™* fan Jonathan Young
(for more from Jonathan, see the end of Chapter 15)

As a new college graduate, I am now no longer living in the dormitory and, therefore, no longer have access to unlimited food! This has caused me to readjust my budget. I quickly realized how much of a drain food was becoming on my funds. The little things add up, and before I knew it, I was nearly out of money. I always considered myself to be frugal, but I have to eat and I'm definitely no Iron Chef in the kitchen. I have come up with little ways to save money on food that can help any college graduate who is trying to stretch their dollar.

For me, a way to save is just packing my own lunch every day. Instead of shelling out my change into vending machines or buying fast food, I pack a sandwich and chips. It seems elementary, but by the end of the week, I'm getting close to five meals for the cost of eating out once. It is hard to totally cut back on going out to eat, but you don't have to. There are plenty of ways to still go out to eat and not spend a fortune.

Little Caesars offers a hot-and-ready pizza for $5 and it's enough for two solid meals. Subway is a healthier alternative with their $5 dollar foot-longs. When I am looking for a break from the mountains of Ramen Noodles that comprise my shelves, these are my first two options.

I know Ramen Noodles and frozen pizza seem like the cliché, but their value is unmatched. A 12-pack of Ramen Noodles costs around $2. Frozen pizzas can be as low as $3. I do get a little sick of Ramen Noodles, but I found that adding canned vegetables (corn, peas) can add a lot to the meal. It's important to shop for deals, use coupons and discounts wherever possible, stick to a shopping list, and never pass up a free meal when it is offered to you!

Another option for eating decently and still saving money is to get together with friends and cook in large portions. Taco Tuesdays, Jambalaya Wednesdays, or grilling burgers is a great excuse to get together with friends and only spend a few dollars.

Saving money on food isn't nearly as challenging as it seems. I think the most important thing to understand is that going out to eat should be substituted with group meals and less expensive restaurants. Food values are all around; it just takes awareness to find them and take advantage of the savings. College graduates have enough financial worries, and these simple tips can help make food less of one.

Chapter 6

THE BENEFITS OF SAVING

"Don't tell me where your priorities are.
Show me where you spend your money,
and I'll tell you what they are."

—James Frick

THERE ARE OTHER BENEFITS of saving besides having a healthy savings account. One benefit of saving is the newly popular, age-old concept of voluntary simplicity. With a simpler life, you have less stuff to shop for, buy, and take care of.

"Voluntary simplicity turns away from activities that have repeatedly failed to deliver satisfaction and contentment... and embraces instead the joys of creativity and community. It celebrates everyday life," explains Dr. April Benson.

We all have too much stuff and too much to do. People who live a simpler life make more time for people than for things. They focus on what really matters to them. What really matters to you? Is it your family, your relationships, your work, your health?

Determine what activities you can cancel and what things you can eliminate. Maybe you can do without that scheduled shopping trip. Instead, you can "go shopping in your own closet" and find some new combinations of clothes you haven't worn for a while. Instead of that expensive dinner date, invite friends over for a convivial potluck. Look for the things that give you pleasure that doesn't involve spending money. Instead of organizing your life around shopping and acquiring, resolve to focus more on one or two simple, no-cost activities that truly give you joy. Make those activities be more of what your life is about.

Sam has a flyer that he copied and shared with friends a few years ago. It reads: "Memories are like a bank account. You withdraw from what you've put in. Deposit a lot of happiness into your bank of memories!" You also have a role in filling the memory banks of your loved ones. Deposit in their accounts and yours, every day of your life. There are "Five Simple Rules for Happiness": 1. Free your heart from hatred. 2. Free your mind from worries. 3. Live simply. 4. Give more. 5. Expect less.

Besides living a simpler and happier life, here are some more benefits of saving:

The opportunity to focus on what really matters

A lack of extra funds for diversion may force you to do things you wouldn't normally do. This isn't always a bad thing. You can take the time to develop genuine friendships that reduce the stress caused by economic hardship. You can take the time to better care for your health through more exercise and meditation. You can discover new, inexpensive activities and hobbies. You can "fall in love all over again" with your family and friends.

Also, you can count your blessings for all that you do have. A simple way to tap into the gratitude font is to, at the end of your day, when you are lying in bed, think back on the events of the past day that you are grateful for. Some people even keep a "gratitude diary." They say it has uplifted them enormously. You can even go on www.GratitudeLog.com and join thousands of active members who write down their "thank you" list.

Major religious organizations also recognize the importance of saving money for a stronger and healthier family life. Ask your church or synagogue financial counseling, training, and materials.

The opportunity to decide "how much is enough"

The concept of "downsizing" has taken on new meaning in recent years. It used to mean moving to a smaller home after living in a larger home and raising a family. Sometimes downsizing is unwillingly imposed due to a job loss, financial, or one of the "d-words," such as death, divorce, disability, or other disaster. As difficult as this transition is, some people have reported that they are surprised to find that they have more time and satisfaction in their simpler lifestyle and say they have been "right sized." The need to downsize has given the opportunity to look at options in new ways that bring lifestyles into line with available resources.

Whenever change is imposed in our lives, it is due to the pain or discomfort of old circumstances falling away and new adaptations forming. Growth is difficult. The new shoots sometimes get trampled. But if we can nurture our new circumstances with the benefit of pre-planning (having enough savings) and a creative, open state of mind, good things can come from bad. Some, like a real estate agent to the rich and famous, take a philosophical approach to their soaring income that takes a dive. He said, "When the ego drives you, it's like it's more, more, and more—nothing is ever enough." He added that he has turned to meditation to try to find serenity and emulate people who are fulfilled with much less.

The opportunity to re-examine wants and needs

One of the concepts that come under scrutiny in these times is the re-evaluation of true needs and wants. The rhetorical question "How much is enough?" is worth asking. Only you can answer that question, not the media or popular culture. Not to be insensitive, but we are asking you if you have food, shelter, family, friends, and opportunities to make your life better? So many people in this world of ours have none of these things. They have nothing to eat, nowhere to sleep, and no hope.

Everyone answers the question, "How much is enough?" in their own way. Some brave souls have committed to a year-long shopping fast. They entirely abandoned their exhausting quest of buying and managing more possessions with their plastic tickets to happiness. When their resolve weakened, they decided they didn't want their children or their friends see them give up. After the year ended, they found themselves permanently willing to focus less on buying and spending. Other people have vowed to not buy new things, and to acquire only that which is reused, retooled, or recycled.

Learning to want what you have is a key to happiness. In a prayer called the "I Pray You Enough" is the line, "I pray you enough gain to satisfy your wanting. I pray you enough loss to appreciate all that you possess." In the continually changing seasons of our lives, take the time to learn the useful life skill of, when necessary, living with less and living contentedly with just "enough."

The opportunity to help others

What if you do not have much to give to others in need these days? There are still many ways that you can still keep your "giving muscles" in shape. As a small, but meaningful example, you can still donate "abandoned items" like the coins that slip under couch cushions. Go to www.couchange.org. The site managers will aggregate small contributions from piggy banks, partially used gift cards, and frequent flyer miles into large, useful sums.

Almost everyone has some unused items that someone else needs. Empty your closets, attic, and garage of clothing, kitchen items, children's toys, and DVDs. Health care equipment is particularly needed in almost every community. Encourage others to join you in this effort. Children have a naturally generous heart. Some children choose to have their birthday gifts be donations to their favorite charity. Or birthday party guests can bring a toy for a disadvantaged child, instead of a gift for the birthday child. Encourage your child to think in this way. The real gift is sharing an awareness with them that there are many children who are less fortunate than they.

Religious leader John Wesley's wise admonition was, "Make all you can, save all you can, give all you can." Even if you do not have cash to give, charities need something that you can give. In some cases, donating time may be even better than cash. You can help in soup kitchens, answer phones, coordinate mailings, and offer an encouraging word or a shoulder to cry on. If you have special skills in counseling, teaching, care-giving, etc., look for the many opportunities to share them. If you are currently between jobs, volunteering will help to keep you busy, active, and involved. "On-the-job" volunteer training can give you experience with managerial, budgeting, public-relations, fund-raising, and communication skills. Also, your volunteering experience enhances your resume and provides opportunities to network with others.

While looking for a job, you could be one of the many "recession angels" out there. You could be like high-end chef Timothy Tucker, who now teaches culinary classes at the Salvation Army and helps cook for 400 people a day at a homeless shelter. Tucker said that his program is "much more magical and special" than his prior jobs at expensive restaurants. "Here we are able to cook great food and use it to heal people's lives," he said, "It's a much bigger thing in life than cooking incredibly beautiful food for people who have a lot of money to pay for it."

The opportunity to help others more effectively

Numerous web sites and groups can help you become more effective in your giving, whether you want to donate your time, talent, or treasure.

In choosing a charity, think about the concepts of cause and consequence. Do you want to donate to help stop the cause of the problem? Or do you want to help stop the consequences of the problem? For example, homelessness is rising in our country. One of the causes of homelessness is unemployment. You could help with an organization that collects and donates professional clothing for people to wear going on job interviews. Or you could decide to try to alleviate some of the consequences of homelessness by helping at a food pantry or a homeless shelter.

Explore sites that help you determine if the charity is legitimate and how effectively it achieves its mission statement. These charity analysis sites include www.BeyondGoodIntentions. com, www.Guidestar.org, www.CharityNavigator.org, www. GlobalGiving.org, www.CharityWatch.org, and www. GreatNonProfits.org. You may be able to obtain city-specific information from local social agencies. Look at the budget of the charity you are considering. What percent of funding goes to actual service programs, as opposed to funding for special events, administration, and raising more funds? An efficient charity will spend less on the latter activities. In the post-Madoff era, it makes sense to find out how much the charity is investing, with whom, on whose advice, and how diversified are the investments.

In your research, be sure to double check the name of the charity. Many charities have similar names. A research fund and a research center are probably two different entities, each with their own specific rating on the analysis sites. To find out about a charity in person, arrange for a tour of the local office or offer to volunteer there. When you donate money to a charity, keep your receipts and documentation and make sure the charity will keep your contact information confidential. You can request to keep your donation confidential if you wish.

In good times and bad, Andrew Carnegie's admonition holds true, "Surplus wealth is a sacred trust that its possessor is bound to administer in his lifetime for the good of the community." Do not, however, put yourself at financial risk by giving too much. Do not forget our continual admonition to "put your own oxygen mask on first."

The opportunity to give for the right reasons

Never assume that what you would want is what someone else would want. Focus on donations that are practical and effective. Sam tells the story of the dress manufacturer who always had the most successful line of gowns every year. He was asked at his retirement banquet what was his secret of creating popular clothes. He explained, "I have my designers bring their gowns in to show my wife and daughters, and whatever they like, we scrub, and whatever they don't like, we run!" Just because you think a charity will want your gift doesn't mean they can actually use it. The best way to find out is to ask.

Sometimes efforts to help can be harmful to the recipient, particularly when it raises expectations and are not followed through. Unfortunately, the effort of doing so is often wasted, although the motivation is good. This effort can be money, time, or resources. You need to use care and preparation in giving gifts. If you are going to do a good deed, be sure that it will result in truly helping the recipient. The satisfaction of a good deed well done is priceless, but the key part is to see that it is well done.

The opportunity to give yourself more "self-care"

When times are difficult, such as in the recent recession, people are forced to learn to instill nurturing and healing behaviors in their lives just to keep going. Prioritizing your own self-care may feel selfish, but, frankly, no one else will do it for you. At some point during difficult times, you may realize, "I need to take better care of myself." Focus some of your attention on self-care and you will enjoy a fuller life and suffer less stress. Self-care doesn't have to be about spending more money. Here are some no-cost ways to take better care of your mind and body:

- Keep a journal as an effective mental health self-care process. If you don't want anyone to read what you write, type it on your computer, read it over, and ponder it. Make note of some action steps that your journal writing inspired. Then delete the journal entry or save it in a locked file. You will be able to be more honest with yourself if you are confident that your thoughts will not fall into the wrong hands.

- Look on the bright side. Whenever something negative happens, ask yourself, "What are three things that are good about this situation?" When you "hear" yourself being self-critical and putting yourself down, also ask yourself, "What are two 'put ups' I can give myself to counteract my 'put downs'?"

- Spend time with friends and family who encourage and uplift you. There is a huge endorphin rush in feeling the affection and caring of others. The way to get this lift is by true connection. Put technology in its proper place. It is a useful aid, but not a replacement for deep interaction with others. Connect with yourself and with others to achieve significant self-care.

- Get some exercise every day. Exercise is one of the very best self-care modalities you can give both your mind and your body. Every study and every doctor says so. You will be motivated as soon as you experience the mental and physical benefits, so give exercise a chance!

REAL LIFE CASE STUDY
"Cutting Back on a Medical School Budget - Part Two"
Written by *TheSmartestWay*™ fan Rebecca Rubin

- *I keep a close inventory of my closet. I only buy new clothes when I need them. I don't buy clothes that aren't versatile, nor aren't high quality, nor that I am not certain I will wear a lot. I never buy something that I'd only wear once. I never go shopping with my friends because it is easy for me to lose sight of the goal, which is to purchase something I need, that I love, and that I will wear often for the best price. I am friendly with a couple of people who work at my favorite stores and they let me know when a sale will be starting. I buy what I need on sale. When I try on clothing, I always think, will this need any alterations or a special accessory to wear? Sometimes these extras make the purchase go over my budget.*

- *I subscribe to emails from www.dailycandy.com about upcoming sample sales, which I often go to when I am in need of new clothing. Shopping this way has been successful. As a result, I've purchased two pairs of $90 designer pants for $10 each. I have also purchased a pair of Miu Miu sandals for $50, which sold for retail at $375. I wear them almost every day. Some people might view $50 for a pair of shoes as expensive, but they are my favorite pair of shoes, and they've remained in good condition for over three years of use. I rarely shop online. And I don't shop on eBay.*

- *I don't dye my hair at all, ever. It might be a different story if my hair was going gray, but I've just learned to accept that I am a brunette. The dyeing of hair is often a disaster and expensive to maintain. When I get my hair cut, I don't get it styled or blown out. I leave with my hair wet or, if no one* is occupying the seat with the hairdryer, I sit underneath it and read until it's dry. I get my hair cut for half the price this way. I go to a stylist who is really good at cutting hair, and I get a great haircut for $35 and I give him a $10 tip. I spoke with the stylist who cuts my hair, and let him know what I could spend, and asked if cutting my hair at this price was possible for him. He said he was more than happy to work with me on negotiating the price. Apparently, he is happy to have one more client rather than one less.

- We don't belong to a gym. We are lucky to live in a warm climate, and we take advantage of the opportunities to hike, walk on the beach, and just be outside. I do yoga independently in my apartment. Occasionally, once every month or so. I will take a yoga class, or a Pilate's class, to make sure I'm doing the postures correctly.

<u>PART II:</u>

TheSmartestWay™
TO SAVE — **IN YOUR**
DAILY LIFE

Chapter 7

SAVING ON FOOD SHOPPING

"Money brings you food, but not appetite;
medicine, but not health."

—Henrico Ibsen

S MART, STRATEGIC grocery shopping will help you save money, eat healthier, and be thinner. Buy real food such as fruits, vegetables, dairy, lean meats, and fish. Do not think you are saving money or nourishing your body by buying more calorie-dense foods, such as sweetened cereals, and packaged foods, such as macaroni and cheese. These items can be loaded with preservatives, sugar, salt, and fat. Read the nutritional chart on the back of the package. If the ingredient list is very long, think twice.

How do you know if food is junk food? If the junk is listed before the food, that is a clue. Avoid products that list Trans Fat as an ingredient. This is the heart-clogging fat. If an item claims it has no sugar, it may contain artificial chemical sweeteners, such as aspartame or Splenda, or sugar alcohols, such as sorbital, xylitol, or malitol, which can affect the digestive system adversely if consumed in large quantities.

Instead of pre-packaged carbs, buy inexpensive bags of whole grains, such as oats, brown rice, and the newly trendy quinoa.

Whole grains reduce the risk of heart disease, diabetes, stroke, and fill you up, but not out. Bags of lentils and beans are also a good source of fiber and protein. Heidi's mom loves to make a delicious, hearty lentil stew. Lentils are inexpensive, delicious, and cook quickly without having to pre-soak like other dried beans. Quinoa is as easy to cook as couscous and even more nutritious. Potatoes are the most adaptable food in the world. Jumbo bags of potatoes or yams will last for weeks.

The average diet contains way too much salt. Sky high sodium levels found in processed foods can raise blood pressure and increase the risk of heart disease and stroke. Fruits and vegetables are delicious and low in sodium. Save money with frozen fruits and vegetables, which are less expensive than fresh produce and may have even more nutrition locked into them.

Don't grocery shop while angry, hungry, tired or in a hurry. You will overspend. Obtain a map of the current layout of your store and coordinate your list by aisle so you can chart an efficient course throughout the store. Decide who in your family should do the shopping. For example, Heidi's husband does a much better job of saving money at the grocery store, so he does the grocery shopping. Be sure to use your store discount card, but if you don't have it with you, just use your phone number to call up the account number.

Clip it

Couponing will save you money. Coupon use is soaring. Partake in the savings trend. Start now and join the crowd. Newspapers, fliers, and mailers have lots of coupons. The Internet has a tornado of coupons at dozens of sites, including www.Coupons.com, www.DealCoupon.com, www.CouponSurfer.com, www.TheGroceryGame.com, www.SlickDeals.com, www.SmartSource.com, www.FindSavings.com, and www.HotCouponDeals.com.

Also check out www.ShortCuts.com, www.BeCentsable.net, www.JumpOnDeals.com,www.AFullCup.com,www.Upromise. com, www.MoneySavingMom.com, and www.CouponMom. com. You can compare prices at www.comparepricesonline. com.

Your favorite grocery store probably has its own coupons. Even high-end markets have coupons in the in-store magazine Whole Deal.You can find coupons at www.WholeFoodsMarket. com and www.WholeFoodsCoupons.net.

You can find a five-step tour on how to access online coupons on www.CouponMountain.com. You can put in the product you want to buy and the word "coupon" and also check out the manufacturer's website for coupons.You will learn how to find coupons quickly and pick up some of the lingo, such as BOGO, which stands for "buy one, get one free." Note: just because a coupon says "Five for $10" does not mean you have to buy five, unless it is specifically stated. You could use the coupon to buy one for $2.

If you have a supermarket "loyalty" card, there is a no-click, no-print way to get discounts. Find the reasonably priced grocery stores in your area, such as Food-4-Less, www.Food4Less. com and The Food Emporium, www.TheFoodEmporium.com. Sign up for free loyalty programs or club cards at multiple grocery stores. You may be able to add the value of coupons directly onto your loyalty card. You can point and click to online coupons and link them with your supermarket loyalty card.You can also receive text messages for deals, click on the message, and the message tells your supermarket to add the discount when you buy the item and swipe your loyalty card at the checkout counter. Also, shoppers can use their phone cameras to scan a product's bar code and instantly find and retrieve a coupon to lower the price. If you forget your card, the cashier may be to access your discount code with your phone number.

Pace yourself with couponing

Sit down at your computer and do a search, "What to cook with…?" or get some of the cookbooks listed in our Suggested Reading List at the back of this book.

If all the options for couponing sound overwhelming, start small. Stephanie Nelson, author of *Greatest Secrets of the Coupon Mom* and other books on coupons, explains three levels of saving on food: busy shopper, rookie shopper, and varsity shopper. If you are busy, use an empty envelope as "coupon central." When you get to varsity level, you can keep your coupons in an accordion checkbook-size organizer that you can buy at a discount store. Keep it in your car so it is always handy. When you are making your grocery list, put "c" by the item if you have a coupon. Bookmark and join a few coupon websites. Take the coupons that are placed on the store shelves next to the discounted item.

In 2009, coupon clippers saved an estimated total of $317 billion! Your co-workers may want to start a coupon box to collect unused coupons to share with each other. Soon couponing will be a normal part of your shopping strategy. If you have children, teach them when they are young. Put your children in charge of finding coupons. As an incentive, give them a percentage of the savings.

The real secret to success is when you get a coupon, use it only for items you would already be planning to buy. Is the coupon craze giving you coupon haze? Coupons save money only if you would initially have bought the item at a higher price. If you were not going to buy the item in the first place, the coupon did not save you money, it helped you spend more money. For example, in the case of a $20 item and a $10 coupon. Sounds like a savings, right? If you were already planning to buy the item, you now saved $10. However, if you wouldn't have bought the item in the first place, the coupon actually cost you $10, right? Keep your coupons in your coupon envelope and go through it periodically. Try to let a cool head prevail.

Use a food calendar

Streamline your food purchases with a customized grocery list and a food calendar. To create a streamlined, super-fast grocery list, write or type the items you frequently buy at the grocery store. Arrange the items in rows according to the aisle they are in at your favorite grocery store. Photocopy the list and post it on your refrigerator. Circle the items you need. When you shop, follow the list. It will be a breeze with no backtracking or wandering. There is even an iPhone app for this called Grocery IQ.

A food calendar will save you time and money. There are two ways to use a food calendar. First, plan your meals throughout the week and the month. Rotate your favorite dishes for variety and so you do not get tired of them. Plan to use the leftovers creatively. For example, roast a chicken (or several) on Monday, make chicken tacos or chicken tortilla soup on Tuesday, make Chinese Chicken Salad or chicken casserole on Wednesday, and make chicken stir-fry or chicken pizza on Thursday. Then cook a roast on Friday and use the leftovers for a beef and potato stew on Saturday and beef tostadas on Sunday.

Use your food calendar to note the best time of the year for buying certain kinds of foods in your part of the country. Find out when your favorite fruits are "in season." Generally, citrus such as oranges and grapefruit usually go on sale in December and January; tomatoes in June; berries, cherries, melons, and peaches in July and August; and autumn vegetables, such as pumpkins, cranberries, sweet potatoes and yams, in October and November. It is no surprise that turkeys go on sale the day after Thanksgiving and hams go on sale the day after Easter. Do not forget that our favorite food group—candy and chocolates—go on sale after Valentine's Day, Easter, and Halloween.

Plan it

Plan your meals ahead by stockpiling great deals on fish, beef, and chicken that you can store or freeze for later. Plan ahead by packing lunches made of leftovers from the night before. There is a blog on packed lunches called www.LunchInABox. net. Plan ahead by throwing some items in a crock-pot slow cooker so dinner will be ready when you come home from work.

The Internet is full of websites under frugal or thrifty meals and meal planning. Lots of cooking and homemaking magazines, such as *Women's Day, Family Circle, Good Housekeeping,* and *Ladies Home Journal,* share quick, healthy, inexpensive meal recipes. For example, a recent edition of *Everyday Food* magazine contained an article entitled, "Five Great Meals, One Short List." The five dinners served four people and the total grocery bill was less than $50.

Plan your grocery shopping trips. Do not shop during times when the store has long lines at the check-out counter. Do not lose track of time; check your watch when you walk in and tell yourself you will be at the checkout counter at a specific time. Do not shop when you are hungry. Comparison shop at local wholesale clubs, co-ops, dollar stores, and big box stores such as Sam's Club and Walmart. Your planning will pay you back.

Track it

Track how much you spend on food. Do you know the approximate amount automatically? If not, there is good news. Whatever the amount is, you can cut it with no hardship. Here's how to do it. Write your best guess of your monthly food budget on an envelope and tape it to the refrigerator. For the next month, each time you go to the grocery store, put the receipt in the envelope. How close was your guess? Now, assign a specific amount that fits your budget. As you become a more strategic shopper, you will be able to trim that amount a bit more next month.

Next month, put your allotted amount in cash into your "Groceries" envelope. Promise yourself you will shop only with cash—the amount in that envelope. To make sure you still have money in the envelope at the end of the month, divide the money into four envelopes, labeled week 1, 2, 3, and 4. Carry that week's grocery envelope with you for that week. When it is empty, use what you have on hand. Go to www.FoodieView. com and type in the items you have in your refrigerator. Up pops some new recipes you can try with those ingredients. If you have leftover money, save it for the end of the month to go out for a treat! Better yet, add it to your savings account. If you are often short by the end of the month, look at what emergencies popped up and figure out how to plan for them next month.

At the checkout counter, check your receipt. Checkout errors are common. Many errors are computer-driven. Items can accidentally be overcharged due to the sale price not being programmed into the system. Human error could cause problems, too, such as items that have the price mislabeled or are shelved under the wrong pricing sign.

Know the right people

Another way to track your grocery shopping is to start tracking down your favorite foods at bargain prices. Be a sleuth. Do you buy a lot of meat, chicken, and fish? Here is a key area where you can save. Befriend the butcher at your grocery store. Ask what days and times he or she is required to mark down the meat. You can get two-for-ones on ground turkey, chicken, cube steak, and pork. Does the butcher do the markdowns at a certain time in the afternoon? It never hurts to ask. Of course, if the meat is about to expire, cook it or freeze it right away. If you open it and it is not fresh enough, return it. If you buy a whole chicken, that is usually less expensive than buying the parts. However, the butcher usually will cut it up for you for free.

You actually pay extra for the butcher's labor on pre-packaged goods. The perfectly trimmed chicken will cost more. You can trim a little fat off yourself. You can find a video online on how to cut up a whole chicken. It can be worth a few moments of your time to save a lot of money over time. The butcher will usually cut up a larger piece of meat or fish at no charge.

Note: The USDA has three categories for beef: prime, choice, and select. The select category is the least expensive and the least fatty. Therefore, it is the best for your wallet and your waist. Tenderize it with a marinade or in the crockpot. Other sources of protein that are delicious and inexpensive are canned tuna and salmon, peanut butter, and soybeans.

Talk to the produce manager at your store. He or she can tell you what days and what time they mark down the produce. They can also tell you when your favorite fruits and vegetables are in season and when you can get the best deals. Plan your grocery shopping trips accordingly.

Co-op it and outlet it

Strength of community is what a co-op grocery store is all about. To find a co-op near you, go to www.coopdirectory. org. Heidi joined a co-op when she was a college student in Boise, Idaho. It was where the cool, hip people hung out. If you live in an agricultural area, you could buy a share in a community-supported agricultural program, called a CSA. At www.LocalHarvest.org, find out more about how you can help pay part of a local farm's operating expenses in exchange for receiving produce. A buying club is another cooperative way to buy food. Members of these clubs, found on www. UnitedBuyingClubs.com, purchase food in bulk and distribute it to other members.

Bakery outlets offer super discounts. If your family likes sandwiches and pastries, bakery outlets are a great place to save on your bread budget. Brand-name baked goods that are near their expiration dates may be 50 percent off.

If you need herbs by the pound, check out www.AtlanticSpice. com on the East Coast and www.SFHerb.com on the West Coast.

Grow it

You can plant a small vegetable and herb garden. Herbs are easy to grow. Basil, rosemary, thyme, and mint tend to be happy in little pots on a sunny window sill. Fresh herbs taste better and cost much less than store-bought herbs. If you have a balcony or patio, you could try container gardening. Find ceramic pots, buckets, and other containers at discount stores and yard sales. You can hand-water the containers or use a drip-irrigation hose. Kits are available at www.EarthBox.com, www.TheGardenPatch.com and www.AeroGarden.com. You may have seen the www.TopsyGardening.com infomercial on television. They have kits for growing tomatoes, hot peppers, and strawberries upside down from a hook on your balcony!

If you venture out to build a garden, start small. Find a sunny, manageable little plot in the back yard. Make sure the area receives sufficient water from your sprinklers. Shovel in a bag of good soil, and plant a few squash, zucchini, or pumpkin seeds and watch them grow. You can buy seeds for a reasonable price at Pinetree Garden Seeds (www.SuperSeeds.com).

If you start having fun, you may want to invest in a raised bed wood frame and fencing to keep grass and animals out of your budding endeavors. Try to get recycled wood for the frames and fencing. See if your city has a free compost site to load up on soil for your garden. You also may find free dirt at your local pool construction company. Call to be put on the list for when they are digging in your area. Websites and television shows are devoted to gardening, such as www.JoeGardener. com, www.garden.org, and www.organicgardening.com.

A communal garden is an alternative to planting a garden in your own backyard. Find out if you can sign up for a plot in one of the many community garden projects sprouting up around the country. Some community gardens have waiting lists for spaces, which can be rented for a monthly or annual fee.

If you grow enough, you can swap with other gardener friends. You can even freeze your bounty or learn how to can it.

Make gardening a family affair

Heidi comes from a family that likes to grow things. Her mother's father was a farmer in Montana all of his life. Her mother, who grew the sweetest corn she has ever tasted, has always kept a small garden. Some of Heidi's happiest childhood memories were when she and her mother worked half the night putting fruits and vegetables into jars before they became overripe. Neighbors' fruit trees would start raining plums, apricots, and peaches, and Heidi's mother would discover full, aromatic bushel baskets waiting on her back step. Through the evening, the kitchen would be warm and lively with the gentle pop-pop-pop of the glass Mason jars sealing after they were removed from the pressure cooker. Late one night, there was no time to take the pits out of the peaches, so she and her mother decided to leave the pits in. Heidi will never forget the spicy, nutty flavor of home-canned, unpitted peaches.

In arid California, Heidi has good luck growing fool-proof zucchinis and tomatoes. She observed that some herbs need lots of care, while others try to take over the garden. For example, mint has a "personality" that needs to be contained. Mint once tried to take over half of her backyard! Nevertheless, you can never have "too much" mint. You can use it for garnish on chicken or desserts, brew it for tea, and freeze it for making fresh mint juleps and mojitos in the summer. Make gardening a family project. Children enjoy watching the magic of a tiny seed growing into something edible and delicious.

When Sam was young during his summers in Michigan, his father negotiated with local growers to allow Sam and his brothers to pick cantaloupes and watermelons left behind by the harvesters in the nearby fields. Then the boys would go door-to-door selling the product to their suburban neighbors. Also, his family's backyard was a vegetable garden. It was his responsibility, along with his brothers, to maintain the garden and sell excess vegetables to neighbors.

REAL LIFE CASE STUDY
"A Crack in the Floor"
Written by *TheSmartestWay*™ fan Barbara S. Cochran

My earliest recollection of the meaning of "saving" came from my mother and father. We lived in England. Mom was a "Lady in Waiting" for a member of royalty, and Dad was the personal valet to King Edward, who abdicated the throne to marry Wallis Simpson. After the King's abdication, my father and mother married, and left their employment with the Royal Family to begin a family of their own.

Dad worked in London at Charter House in the Food Service Department, and my mom was a "stay-at-home" mom and pregnant with my brother. Money was tight. Dad was drafted into the Royal Navy in 1940. He and my mom had rented a flat in London. I was probably about four years old and I remember Dad coming home on leave before being shipped out and they were discussing money and counting what they had between them.

I remember sitting on a chair at the table and playing with some of the coins. A half-crown piece fell to the floor and rolled into a crack in the floor. My Mom and Dad immediately began digging around to get it back. Ultimately, they pulled up the floorboard and retrieved the half-crown. Not long after that, Dad was shipped out. The following years were tough for Mom, and after the war ended, Dad made the decision to bring the family to the U.S. for a better life.

We arrived in the U.S. in 1947 and settled in South Carolina with the friends who had sponsored Dad to bring us to the U.S. He immediately left for North Carolina to start a new job. Mom, my brother, and I followed about a year later once enough had been saved for a place to live.

As you can see, my lesson on "saving" came very early in life. I have always felt the need to "count pennies." It wasn't always easy to put extra aside, but I worked as a young girl in school and in college. Once I married and had children, I tried to instill in them the need to "watch your pennies." Now that they are married and have families of their own, they are teaching their children how to save, too.

I can say now that life is great. Money isn't a problem anymore, and I am thankful for my lessons on "saving" to Mom and Dad. They taught me well.

Chapter 8

SAVING ON FOOD HANDLING

"I know the price of success: dedication, hard work, and an unremitting devotion to the things you want to see happen."

—Frank Lloyd Wright

AFTER YOU BRING food home from the store, you can still save money by storing it in ways that makes it last longer. To throw food away is to throw money away. For example, keep lettuce fresh longer by rinsing and drying it thoroughly before bagging it. Some fruits, such as strawberries, will wilt if washed too soon before eating. Wash them just before using. Store apples in the refrigerator, and freeze fruits and vegetables if you cannot use them right away. Onions and garlic last longer at room temperature, but other foods last longer chilled. Buy a large bag of potatoes and store it in a cool dry area.

What to do with leftovers? Think soups, stews, smoothies, frittatas, stir-frys, pizzas, pastas, and tortilla wraps. Throw extra vegetables into a pot to make stew stock. Throw vegetables into the blender to make a creamy soup. Toss extra fruit and yogurt into a blender to make a smoothie. Keep ends of loaves of bread and put them in the blender or food processor to make bread crumbs. Put all leftovers in a plastic bag with the date marked on it. Inexpensive plastic, sealable bags, and storage containers can be found at dollar stores and IKEA. You could designate one shelf of the refrigerator to leftovers so you can keep track of them easier.

Wash it

The USDA's organic certification process is very expensive for farmers. Organically grown foods can be 10 percent to a 100 percent more expensive. Fortunately, organic foods are available widely at almost everywhere food is sold. We suggest that you not pay organic prices for fruits and vegetables that have a removable skin, such as such as potatoes, carrots, avocados, bananas. The skin protects the food from much of the pesticides. Instead, wash your produce with a "veggie wash." This cleans your food without a soapy aftertaste.

Of course, healthy food is important. You can inquire at the farmers' markets about their farming methods. At the grocery store, you have to try to decipher the codes. "Organic" dairy, beef, and poultry come from animals that were fed organic feed and not given hormones or antibiotics. "Raised without antibiotics" and "hormone-free" means just that. "Free-range" means that the animal was given daily open-air access, but keep in mind that only five minutes outdoors on a concrete slab is enough to qualify. If your love for animals reaches into your wallet, you can find meat, dairy, and eggs that are "certified humane," meaning they were raised with sufficient space and normal activity. Whole Foods has plans to roll out its own similar label, "Animal Compassionate."

Wash your apples well because they are considered the most polluted produce. See a full list of the Working Group's Dirty Dozen list at www.ewg.org. Wild Pacific salmon is cleaner than farmed Atlantic salmon. The canned version is less expensive. Avoid milk that contains the hormone rBST (or rBGH), which is banned in the European Union and Canada.

Some foods are best to buy organic. However, some foods are not worth paying more for organic. Do not pay more for brown eggs. They are identical to white eggs. Do not pay more for "hormone-free" eggs. The use of hormones in poultry has been banned for decades. Do not pay more for organic beef. For better beef that is sometimes cheaper, look for "grass-fed" beef.

Freeze it

The USDA has a shocking statistic, which is that the average household wastes between 10 to 40 percent of their food. That can really add up! Learn how to buy the right amount and how to store leftovers. If you buy in bulk, divide it and freeze it. Make extra batches on the weekend and freeze them in individual containers. Instead of baking or grilling one chicken, make a whole tray.

Would a freezer save you money in the long run? Here are some of the foods you can freeze: baked potatoes, cheese, casseroles, meats, sausage, bacon, bell peppers, and bags of frozen vegetables and fruit. You can also freeze bread items, such as waffles, bagels, muffins, pastries, cookies, tortillas, and loaves of breads. The nice thing about frozen foods is that you thaw only what you need, so there is no waste. When you cook ground beef or cubed chicken, make extra and freeze it in small portion bags for use in other dishes later. You can thaw and toss it into chili, tacos, pizza, and casseroles. For dessert, stock up on popsicles and ice cream when they go on sale, or better yet, make your own.

You can keep a container of meat bones, onion tops, and carrot peelings. These can be frozen and later simmered to make soup stock. Almost-spoiled vegetables can be roasted in the microwave and then frozen. This mixture can be added to lasagna, stews, pizzas, and casseroles.

Stretch it

Find new meals that you or your family will like that cost less. Recipe websites with budget-conscious meals include www.AllRecipes.com, www.EatingWell.com, and www.taste.com. Cutting back on portion size overall is an effective way to trim your budget as well as your waistline.

Make more salad entrees. Use more chicken and turkey. To cut back on the expense of meat, use less meat and more vegetables or pasta in casseroles and entrees. You can cut back a few ounces of the meat in almost any recipe and no one will notice the difference. That's saving calories and cents. Potatoes, pasta, and rice are filling, but low-fat side dishes for dinner. Make large casseroles of scalloped potatoes and pots of pasta or rice. (Heidi thinks that brown rice is more delicious, nutritious, and filling than white rice.) The leftovers can be used in your entrée or side dish for the following night. Breakfast is the most important meal of the day. For hearty breakfasts for your family, make a pot of delicious, steel-cut oatmeal. It will last in the refrigerator for a week. Non-fat powdered milk tastes like skim milk and is less expensive. Loose leaf tea in a box and coffee in a can is less expensive than individual packets.

Every year, www.Costco.com publishes a new discount meal cookbook. The 99 Cents Only store also has its own cookbook. You can buy used copies of these cookbooks at the store or online. In the Suggested Reading section at the back of this book lists many more titles. Do not fall victim to the so-called Costco-effect that makes people buy larger quantities than they can easily use. You have to be disciplined when shopping in big box stores or you may buy more than you need.

Here is one of the easiest ways to stretch your grocery dollars: Skip the junk food. Do not buy soft drinks and sugary beverages. Drink just pure fruit juices with a little extra water mixed in so they are not so sweet. Seltzer or tonic water is a better alternative to sodas, especially if you add some lemon, lime, or other flavorings. If you think you might be addicted to sodas, cut down gradually. You may get headaches at first, which simply indicate that your body is going through withdrawal from your chemical dependence. You will feel better and look better after you kick the habit. You also will not have to see your dentist as often, which is built-in savings.

If you like wine, which is a healthy food for your heart, try "Two Buck Chuck" wine and other low-cost, but high quality wines from Trader Joe's. Talk with the sales associates at liquor stores and World Market stores sales about low-priced, quality brands on sale. You can get an $8 bottle that is as good as a $20 bottle. The larger liquor stores, such as Beverages and More, now called BevMo www.BevMo.com, often have specials. Ask what's on special for that day.

Try it

Be flexible about brands and try less expensive brands. Try generic brands. Be adventurous. Most stores will let you return their store brand items if you do not like them as much as the name brand version. Try the selection and the store brands in the grocery sections of Super Walmart, www.WalMart.com, SuperTarget, www.Target.com, and Kmart, www.Kmart.com. If there is a Trader Joe's www.TraderJoes.com in your area, you must visit to see the creatively presented variety of reasonably priced foods. It is like a gourmet shop that is very affordable. Heidi and her husband shop at their local Trader Joe's at least once a week. If you have never been to a Costco or visit www.Costco.com, you will be surprised by the high quality of the bakery and deli counters, and the fish, chicken, and meats. Wholesale clubs, such as Costco and Sam's Club www.SamsClub.com, have an annual membership, so take into account how much you will save each year to see if it is worth it for how much you spend.

Try new ways of eating. Try "breakfast for dinner" such as a frittata with bacon. Be creative with whatever veggies, meats, or cheeses you have on hand. Grill and put them into a flour tortilla to make a quesadilla. Throw them in with some eggs to make an omelet. Throw them in with some lettuce to make a salad. Try a "leftovers buffet dinner" to clear out the leftovers in the refrigerator. Try new recipes. Use what is in the refrigerator and see what happens.

The wonderful phrase "Necessity is the mother of invention" means that you can become an inventive cook. Famous chefs don't cook things the same way as everyone else or they wouldn't be famous. They try creative replacements, sometimes because that's what they have available. Have you ever looked at a menu with unusual combinations of ingredients and said to yourself, "I never thought of that!" Don't be afraid to ask yourself, "What if?" and let the contents of your cupboards and refrigerator inspire you.

If you have never tried a crock pot slow cooker, now is the time. Crock pots tenderize less expensive cuts of meats, such as extra-lean beef stew meat. Crock pots make larger meals and use less electricity than the stove or oven. Best of all, they are easy. You can find crock pot entree recipes on sites such as www.BusyCooks.about.com, www.Food.aol.com, www.Food.com, www.RecipesToGo.com, and www.TheSimpleDollar.com.

An inexpensive air popper makes fresher and healthier popcorn than you could ever buy. If you want to try your hand at making your own yogurt and cream cheese from powdered milk, how-tos are on www.TheFamilyHomestead.com and www.HopefulHousewife.com. If you are short on time, try meals made with store-bought packaged or prepared ingredients with recipes by Sandra Lee at www.SandraLee.com, www.FoodNetwork.com, and www.SemiHomemade.com. "We have a triple-A factor," Sandra Lee says, "It has to be aspirational, accessible, and affordable."

Stockpile it

You will be prepared for last-minute meals if you stock up on staples that you always use. Cans of beans, tomatoes, tomato sauce, soup, chicken, fruit, and tuna; boxes of potato buds, powdered milk, and pancake mix; and bags of brown rice and pasta are good to have on hand. Good snack foods to have in the pantry are pretzels, crackers, peanut butter, and brownie mix. To avoid overeating, keep your stockpile of snack foods in a separate area or you may find yourself finishing off bags of goodies in front of the television every night! These days, overeating and obesity is a serious concern.

Speaking of buying in bulk, avoid small, snack-pack packaging. You can buy in bulk and pop the smaller servings into your own plastic bags. Packaging can account for more than 50 percent of the cost of food items. Therefore, it makes sense that you can save money by shopping in the bulk bins at grocery stores. You can also save by shredding your cheese, washing your lettuce, peeling your carrots, and chopping your fruit. A few minutes a week could add up to quite a tidy sum of accumulated savings over a year.

REAL LIFE CASE STUDY
"Getting Back to Basics"
Written by *TheSmartestWay*™ fan Myriam-Rose Kohn
President of www.jedaenterprises.com

There must be a reason why magazines such as "Real Simple" are making a return. While I had to stay in a hotel last year, I saw someone on television showing how to make a peanut butter and jelly sandwich. Was this for real? It seems that an entire generation has lost the art of even simple cooking. Never mind preparing a scrumptious meal. My students often inform me how they frequently eat at fast food places because that is all their parents can "afford."

It's time to get back to basics both money-wise and health-wise. The money spent at a fast food place can be better spent on real food. Families should make healthy eating a priority over entertainment. When finances are really tight, which is more important, your health or premium channels on your television? I think it's odd when the television bill does not get trimmed when that savings could easily provide healthy meals for at least a week for a family on a low budget.

If you are short on cash, you can purchase a pre-cooked chicken for $6 and a 10 lb. bag of potatoes for $4 (often on sale at a buy-one-get-one free price). The potatoes would be enough for a few other meals, and the money saved from not buying beverages can be invested into buying fresh vegetables and juice at considerable savings. You not only actually save money, but your family is also eating healthier, because eating fewer preservatives will cause less disease.

You can work wonders with a loaf of bread, eggs, and cheese as well. The number of ways in any combination these can be used is endless. Vary it with different vegetables and you will still beat fast food prices while providing healthier nutrition for your family.

If you don't even know how to boil an egg, many courses are offered quite inexpensively. If all else fails, watch a cooking show for beginners on the Food Channel. PBS also offers cooking shows. As a parent, whether you work or not, simple meals can be prepared while involving the children. Teach them life skills that they will need as adults.

You may also want to consider buying meat from a butcher rather than from a market, if you're not a vegetarian, of course. It may seem that you are paying more at the time, sometimes up to $2 a pound more; however, you probably will end up with less fat, so you are ahead of the game, both money- and health-wise.

Fresh fruits and vegetables do not cost any more at a farmers' market than at the market. More often than not, they are more flavorful and have the added benefit of not having had as many insecticides sprayed on them. You can find a directory of farmers markets at www.ams.usda.gov, which is the USDA's Agricultural Marketing Service's website.

There are healthy and inexpensive cleaning products, too. For example, vinegar is a great cleaner for your sinks and tiles in the shower, on counters, and on floors. As a matter of fact, it is highly recommended by the people who sell and lay the tiles. You can buy one gallon of vinegar for about $4 at stores like Costco and Sam's Club. While some people may not like the odor, vinegar will not harm you if you inhale it, nor will it harm your children or pets.

Chapter 9

SAVING ON WHAT CLOTHES TO BUY

"Whoever loves money never has money enough."
—Proverbs 23:4

WE HAVE A CHAPTER on clothes in our first book, but this topic continually demands attention. Many Americans seem to focus on their clothes more than any other possessions. From a philosophical viewpoint, clothes are simply a uniform to qualify a person to be in a specific situation. They are a message, "Yes, I know who I am and where I am, and yes, I should be here." In another sense, they are a costume that we wear to say who we are, and how we feel about ourselves.

During her many years in the women's fashion industry as a reporter, editor, fashion show consultant, and a personal shopper, Heidi focused intently on the creative and commercial aspect of clothing. Maybe her career path was launched when, as a little girl, she had to select her clothes from the JCPenney catalog because she was a "chunky girl" size that wasn't carried in the brick-and-mortar stores. Eventually, as an adult, she began to view an obsession with fashion as a time-consuming and expensive distraction. Bear in mind, fashion comes and goes. Style lasts forever.

Before you shop for clothes, you need to know what you need. Before you know what you need, you need to know your style. What you buy is based on your style. Everyone can develop their own style, as they try a variety of shapes, color combinations, and fashion trends, and find what looks best on them. Find your own style by searching magazines and catalogues for ideas. When possible, tear out pages that you like and glue them onto a poster board. These collages are sometimes called "vision boards."

Soon, a uniting theme will appear. Use your vision board to analyze your wardrobe and develop a cohesive list of the specific pieces you are missing. Put together your completed wardrobe carefully, piece by piece. This wardrobe will work for you under all circumstances, and it will enhance the new pieces that you add in later.

Organize your closet

Before you go shopping for more clothes, be sure you know what you already have. There are several ways to organize your closet. One of the best ways is by color and shape. For example, all the dark pants together and all the dark jackets together. That way you can see what you are missing.

You may have looked into a closet full of clothes and said to yourself, "I have nothing to wear!" Maybe you actually don't have the appropriate outfit for certain occasions. Make a list of what you need to complete your work outfits and casual outfits. Shop for those items, and those items only, on sale, and during the appropriate season.

The best way to deal with the question, "What should I wear?" is to plan ahead. Heidi always lays out her clothes the night before. For some reason, in the mornings, her "fashion mojo" is not fully functioning and her last-minute wardrobe choices are not always the best. Match the lead time to the need. If you are going on a week-long trip, allow a week to start laying out your clothes so you can create a streamlined grouping.

Take a look at your wardrobe. Is it working for you, or are you working for it? When your clothes have synergy and work together, they will give you far more options, freedom, and creativity. Structure supports freedom. So think of it this way. The time and money you save allows you more time to be creative with what you already own. Take control of your closet and learn to enjoy it rather than struggle with it.

Rediscover the classics

A core wardrobe of basic colors and classic styles is not only elegant and timeless, but also makes life simpler. It is more practical, easier to mix-and-match, and less expensive than outfits that can only coordinate with each other. You could even be very minimalist and avoid prints. Find excellent quality that will enhance your accessories.

"Investment dressing" is timeless, classy, and economical. A consistent style in your wardrobe enhances your personal image. It also requires fewer clothes. Choose clothes that will be classically, elegantly "you" for years to come. When in doubt, choose the simple, timeless, and understated.

We suggest that you can dress both elegantly and economically. Tim Gunn, the fashion critic on Lifetime's television show, "Project Runway," was asked how the average person can navigate their way through runway trends to find pieces that work in real life. His response was, "I don't believe in chasing trends. Please have the confidence to embrace a seasonal on-trend item, providing it suits your taste and lifestyle, and eschew everything else." That is just like we said.

Here is a list of timeless classic pieces and accessories for professional women. Great shapes are sweater sets, long cable knit cardigans, straight sheath dresses, wrap waist dresses, pleated trousers, turtle necks, crew neck t-shirts, buttoned blouses, dress shirts, A-line skirts, and blazers. Best fabrics are no-wrinkle or pressed cotton, silk, and wool. The best prints are plaids, stripes, dots, paisleys, and some animal prints. Shoes are always a challenge, so look for loafers, pumps, spectator toe, ballet flats, and classic boots, all in smooth or crock leather. Belts and handbags are in your core neutral color in smooth or crock leather. For cold weather, wear dark tights and long muffler shawls. A basic earring wardrobe includes pearl or diamond studs, silver studs, gold studs, silver hoops, and gold hoops. Simple necklaces are in silver chain, gold chain, and pearl strands.

For evening, Heidi likes patent leather black ballet flats and patent leather black crock loafers. Accessories are gold with rhinestones or silver with rhinestones. She has a small quilted, Chanel-look black leather bag with chain strap to go with gold accessories or a black beaded clutch. For a professional weekend style, wear cotton, wool or suede slacks in black, white or tan with crew neck or turtle-neck tops in your palette of colors. You can add edgier print jackets, leather jackets, denim jackets, shawls, fun shoes and accessories to make your look more casual.

Find your fashion muse

European women are admired for their individual and timelessly classic look. They choose fewer items, of higher quality, for their closet. They choose the classics and individualize them. Rather than buying lots of trendy things, they buy a few excellent pieces and wear them for years. They accessorize them with more current pieces. It's all about restraint. Coco Chanel once said, "Elegance is refusal." In 1985, Donna Karan introduced the concept of Essentials—seven easy pieces that every woman should have in her closet. They were comfortable, classic, elegant, packable, and interchangeable. They are still classics today, and she has remained an inspiration to professional women for decades.

Who inspires your fashion sense? Who is your fashion muse? Tim Gunn points out that, from a man's perspective, "It's important for each of us to have a fashion mentor, someone whose fashion and style we admire and to whom we can look for spiritual guidance, as in, 'Would so-and-so wear this?' I have two mentors, Cary Grant and George Clooney. They never fail me!"

Classics for men don't have to cost a fortune. Shop for classic styles at vintage shops. Heidi's husband buys his cufflinks at a vintage shop in Hollywood at a significant discount. Burlington Coat Factory has classic styles for men, such as silk pastel power ties, dress shoes, and all-cotton French-cuff dress shirts for business, and khakis, golf shirts, black mock-neck sweaters, and microfiber bomber jackets for casual Fridays. Men should avoid showing their legs in the workplace, so they should make sure that their socks are long enough. Extra-long dress socks for men can be found at Burlington Coat Factory www. BurlingtonCoatFactory.com, Stein Mart www.SteinMart.com, Nordstrom Rack, shop.nordstrom.com/c/nordstrom-rack, and even sometimes at 99Cents Only Stores www.99only.com.

Build in your creativity

Build a wardrobe that is useful, unique, and makes you look and feel great. As you develop your own personal wardrobe style, you'll learn to "brand" your individual look and enjoy dressing and shopping. For even more individuality, you can make your own customized clothes. Women can design their own clothes and accessories with instructional videos called Self-Made Girl at www.ElleGirl.com, the teen offshoot of *Elle* magazine.

Use all your garments in every possible way. Make shirts do double duty as light jackets. Women, make sleeveless dresses do double duty as jumpers.

Heidi enjoys making her clothes more unique by switching to more upscale, intriguing buttons that can easily transform a garment. For shoes that have laces, she switches to satin or velvet ribbons for a more festive or dressy look.

Let color define your look

Both men and women can base their wardrobe on two neutral colors that form the "core" of their wardrobe. Make sure that you have trousers, blazers, and shoes (and skirts and handbags for women) in those two colors. For business, white shirts go with everything for both men and women. For casual, white or sand-colored slacks go with everything. Then add variety with colored shirts, tops, and sweaters.

Heidi recently simplified her wardrobe by choosing black and warm beige as her two neutral core colors. Beige is a very versatile color in all its shades from light honey (ivory) to almost camel. This color always looks great with the other core neutrals of black, brown, navy, or gray. Do not choose a non-neutral as the core of your wardrobe. Bright colors tend to go in and out of fashion quickly. As the beautiful, ageless model Iman was quoted as recommending, "Own lots of neutrals and a few great-color pieces. You will get more mileage out of your grays, blacks, navies, camels, and whites."

Heidi's second recommendation is to choose two main accent colors, one from the blue and green family and one from the red family. Heidi has blue eyes, so she gravitates toward shades of blue such as teal and sky blue. If you have green or brown eyes, you may prefer all shades of green, such as forest and sage. For your red family accent color for business attire, women look most professional in dark reds, such as burgundy and wines. For casual, mix in some reds, pinks, and corals.

Make sure your colors play nicely together

Everything in your closet should play nicely together. Build a "hard working" and yet creative wardrobe by being disciplined about which colors you buy. Arrange your closet this way: all the tops grouped by color, all the pants grouped by color, etc.

This makes it easier to see what you have. Take photos of all your favorite looks, fully accessorized, and put the photos in a binder. This will help you when you need to pull an outfit together in a hurry.

To enhance your creativity and ease of dressing, be disciplined about which fashion accent colors you choose. Fashion colors, such as limes, fuchsias, oranges, and purples, are best for men in inexpensive accessories such as ties. Women can wear those fashion colors in scarves, shawls, jewelry, socks, wallets, and belts. You can mix them into your casual or weekend wardrobe.

Men generally have an easier time coordinating their colors than women. If everything mixes and matches, a man can create a sufficient wardrobe for a casual office with just a half a dozen pants, shirts, and ties, topped with a few blazers. Color is nearly impossible to match from memory. Bring the item you want to match when you go shopping.

Try this experiment for the next six months to establish your professional image: Resolve that you will buy clothes for the office only if they are in your core colors. Soon you will be amazed at how everything will start working together. Now you will be able to buy better quality clothes and keep them longer. Year after year, as you maintain your commitment to your core colors, your closet will become a happy, organized place in which all the pieces play nicely together.

Black is always in style

Black is always in fashion and it is never boring. It plays well with every color in the rainbow and inspires creativity. Black always looks classic and expensive. It also helps you create a minimal wardrobe. If everything you buy mixes and matches with black, you will need fewer clothes. Men need a black suit, black mock-neck sweaters, and black loafers and dress shoes. Women who need a work wardrobe should have a black pant suit, a black slim skirt, a black Coach-style leather handbag, black lower-heeled pumps, dress boots, and dressy loafers.

For evening, every woman needs an LBD, a little black dress. It can be dressed up for evening with a rhinestone brooch, dressed down with a denim or leather jacket and a scarf, or worn to work with a string of pearls. The LBD is, as they say in Fashionland, a "must have." Do you need proof? The most famous LBD was the Givenchy version worn by Audrey Hepburn in the movie "Breakfast at Tiffany's." In 2006, the dress sold at auction for more than $800,000. Obviously, the LBD is the dress for all time. You can buy an LBD for less than $50 or $100 in many stores.

REAL LIFE CASE STUDY
"Tips on Adjusting to Divorce"
Written by *TheSmartestWay*™ fan Lisa Berg

After my divorce, in a horrid economy with soaring gas prices, I knew it was time to do a serious review of my finances to find solutions that would stop me from using credit cards and enable me to live within my means.

First, I kept record of my spending to the penny for two months and reviewed my utility bills from this past year. I then wrote a budget. By doing just these two things, I was able to get a clear idea of where I was spending too much and where I could save money so that I could stop adding to my debt. I made some quite significant changes in my spending habits:

- *I use direct deposit. Once I see my income in my checking account, I immediately transfer 20 percent of that to my emergency savings fund.*

- *I now use cash for my weekly grocery allowance. If I find myself at the checkout counter exceeding my cash, I remove items from my cart until I have spent at or below that figure.*

- *I allocate 20 percent of my income for miscellaneous spending; i.e., for items I do not need, but would like to have, like design magazines, and beads with which I make jewelry (my two addictions!) and withdraw this amount of cash each month. Once this is gone, I cannot spend more on my "desires."*

- *I cut up all my credit cards with one exception. I use the remaining card only to purchase gasoline. I pay it off monthly. This ensures that I will have no accrued interest charges and, at the same time, helps improves my credit score bit by bit.*

- *I see a number of doctors. Though many wish to see me more often, I've set up my appointments so that I spend in co-pays only the amount that I know will fit within my monthly budget.*

- *I also buy generic medicines wherever possible, and when I find a new prescription costs a fortune, I hold the order and ask my physician if there is something similar which costs less. Often, a substitute can be found.*

- *I subscribe to Internet companies (e.g. www.Groupon.com, www.Flycoupon.com) that offer "daily deals" in my town. I pay half price for many things this way—movie tickets, sandwiches, and, most recently, I paid $20 for an oil change that normally costs $40!*

- *I shop for some of my clothing at thrift stores like Goodwill where I usually find fabulous deals. At Goodwill, I can even find new-with-tag, never-even-worn designer clothing items!*

- I learned how to say "no" to my teenager when he asks for unnecessary things, which has, perhaps, been my greatest challenge!

- I'm seriously considering changing from my Cox Cable bundle to Direct TV or Dish Network. Cox costs $200 per month whereas the others cost about $120 per month. (I can't change yet, I'm waiting for landlord approval.)

- I shop for some of my Christmas gifts year-round because I can look for sales and make purchases if I feel they will be good gifts to give family and friends.

Each month, I browse through Sam and Heidi's book, **TheSmartestWay™ to Save, Why You Can't Hang onto Money and What to Do About It** to discover even more great tips on spending. I feel it is necessary to be mindful of all my spending and to continually search for new ways to save. Their book has helped me put into place a budget that works for me, and it has helped me discover resources I had never heard of before. I am quite thankful for the effort they put into this!

Chapter 10

SAVING ON WHERE TO BUY CLOTHES

*"Whoever said money can't buy happiness
simply didn't know where to go shopping."*

—Bo Derek

HUNDREDS OF STORES in one location can be an overwhelming prospect. Don't let your desire for bargains at the outlet mall blind you to what you really want, which is value. Spending the cost of the product doesn't mean you are "earning" the savings. Saving 50 percent is great, but if you don't need the item, you would be saving 100 percent instead.

How does one make shopping into a saving experience, not a buying experience? First, do your homework: make a list, plot your map, and plan your strategy. Compare the stores in the outlet malls near you by researching online and checking out www.TangerOutlet.com, www.PremiumOutlets.com, and www.PrimeOutlets.com. As Steven Tanger, the CEO of Tanger Factory Outlet Centers, said, "In good times, people like a bargain. In rough times, they need a bargain." You can find discount alternatives for high-end merchandise at outlets for J. Crew, Eddie Bauer, Coach, Polo Ralph Lauren, Florsheim, and American Eagle.

You will be wowed when you visit the outlet of high-end stores such as Off 5th (Saks Fifth Avenue), Nordstrom Rack, Barneys New York Outlet, Last Call Store (Neiman Marcus), which is located in a discount mall south of Las Vegas, along with a St. John Outlet, which also has a store near Palm Springs.

Sometimes regular retail stores have better sale prices and better merchandise. Just because a store says that an item was originally priced high doesn't mean that it actually was. A flimsy T-shirt with a designer label is still a flimsy T-shirt. When you buy from these stores, as when you buy from any store, check the construction of the clothes, including the seams, zippers, and comfort when sitting and walking.

If you are planning a trip, check online at the visitor's bureau for traveler discounts. For example, Macy's offers all out-of-state shoppers a 10 percent discount and free shipping if you show your identification. When you arrive in a new city and stay at a hotel, ask the hotel concierge or front desk agents if they have any shopping tours, shopping coupons, or pamphlets and travel guide booklets. These often contain coupons and deals.

Don't be a discount store snob

If you shop with friends, what kind of friends are they? Do they have the same type of budget you have? Or do they spend more freely? Watch out for financial "frenemies." Do they assure you that "everything will be fine," and that "you deserve to treat yourself," or is it "just too bad" that you can't join them in the fun of shopping beyond your means. If your friends are well-intentioned, they will encourage you to do the right thing for you. They won't make you feel guilty, jealous, or insufficient.

Heidi used to have friends who thought they were "too good" to shop anywhere but department stores and boutiques. If you know what you want and you find it at a great price, what's not to like? After she showed them her discount store finds, they finally decided to sneak into a discount store. They came out beaming. Our advice is, do not be a discount store snob. For example, you can pay a fortune for pantyhose or you can shop at Walmart. The only pantyhose that Heidi likes are from Walmart, the George house brand. They come in long size, which fits her well. The $4 price is an added bonus.

You will be amazed what is out there. Here are some more stores we did not mention in our first book: Neiman Marcus Last Call www.NMLastCallClearanceCenter.com, Century 21 www.c21stores.com, Filene's Basement www.FilenesBasement. com, and Off Broadway Shoes www.OffBroadwayShoes.com. If (and only if!) you have enough self-control, you might consider signing up online for early notice of sales and deals on these websites. Some Loehmann's Stores www.Loehmanns.com even offer no-fee personal shoppers. Frugal fashionistas have rediscovered the newly chic Payless www.Payless.com and Dress Barn www.DressBarn.com. Target www.Target.com has featured offerings from top clothing designers, such as Isaac Mizrahi and Missoni.

Take advantage of customer service survey discounts

Stores such as JC Penney www.JCPenney.com, Banana Republic www.BananaRepublic.com, and the Gap www.gap. com will send you a coupon in return for filling out a customer-service survey. The Limited www.TheLimited.com gives you a coupon if you "like" the store on Facebook. It takes a few moments, and yes, you are disclosing your email address, but if you are a huge fan of the store, you may not mind developing a coupon-rewarding relationship.

A brief dictionary of discount terms

Here are some kinds of discount stores:

Outlet: store that sells at discounted or clearance prices

Flea Markets and Swap Meets: a variety of vendors that sell from rented areas

Consignment: a store that sells your merchandise for you and gives you a percentage of the sale

Thrift: a store that sells second-hand items

Warehouse: a no-frills store or megastore with volume packaging

Here are some kinds of discount merchandise:

Seconds: have cosmetic or functional flaws

Floor Samples: have been used for displays

Irregulars: contain very minor imperfections

Liquidated Stock: stock sold below wholesale price for quick cash

Freight-Damaged Goods: damaged during shipment

Job Lots: gathered for sale as one unit

Odd Lot: left over from wholesalers

Overruns, Overstock or Surplus: excess beyond the amount ordered

Past Season: left over from last season

Samples: shown to buyers, but not for sale

Shop at thrift and consignment stores

Thrift stores are second-hand stores like Goodwill, Salvation Army, and local stores run by churches, hospitals, shelters, and other nonprofits. One in six adults now shops at these stores. More new ones are popping up in upscale communities.

Consignment stores, which sell your items for you and give you a percentage of the sale, often have worthwhile merchandise. Heidi's favorite consignment store purchase is a gray pleated skirt she bought more than 25 years ago for $25. Since then, she has had it shortened, and still wears it often. Second-hand or thrift stores, consignment stores, and exchange stores are refreshing alternatives to the mall. The items are gently "pre-owned" and the prices are amazing!

The latest fashion trend is a casual, mismatched, "thriftyshoppy" look. Retro, slightly worn-looking, vintage looks are similar to pricey stores such as Anthropologie. Secondhand or thrift stores sell donated goods and donate the money to support charities, such as Goodwill, Salvation Army, and local Assistance League stores. Consignment stores sell other people's merchandise in exchange for a portion of the sale. The exchange stores let your exchange your clothes for other clothes in the store.

Thrift and consignment stores are getting new attention and fresh inventory. The National Association of Resale and Thrift Shops estimates there are more than 25,000 thrift stores in the country. The number of these shops increased by seven percent last year. Goodwill stores have enjoyed a compound annual growth rate of 10 percent, and Salvation Army has increased sales by four percent every year since 2007 and. Plug in your zip code at www.narts.org or www.TheThriftShopper. com to find some near you. The most affluent areas have the best stuff. Heidi did a search for thrift shops, vintage shops, and consignment stores in the Los Angeles area. Up popped 20 pages of lists on www.yelp.com and www.yahoo.com. Local high-end magazines frequently feature new designer consignment stores favored by various actresses. Designer consignment at www.therealreal.com offers free pickup if you live in select major cities. It pays you 70 percent of the selling price after you achieve $1,500 in sales.

To save money on your thrift store buys, become well-versed in stain removal tips. Learn how to sew on buttons and mend hems. Don't pass up good buys just because they need a bit of repair. If you are creative and like to sew, drag out your old sewing machine and let loose.

For yard sales and estate sales, focus on the larger sales and ones in better neighborhoods. Most cities have estate sale promoters who will be glad to put you on their mailing list. Look for more information at www.TLCEstateSales.com and www. AuctionGuide.com. Sample sales can be found in large cities with fashion districts, such as Los Angeles, Dallas, Chicago, and New York. Search for sample sales on www.DailyCandy.com.

Make money at consignment stores

If you have nice clothes and accessories you no longer want, take them to a local consignment store. First, clean them up and repair them. You will get a better price than at a garage sale. Present them to the consignment store owner in their best condition, without wrinkles, stains, or damage. The owner will select some of your items, put them on the sales floor, and send you a percentage of the sales price if the items sell within a month or two. The items that are not sold can be donated or returned to you.

In our first book, we mentioned that staying the same weight helps reduce the amount of money you spend on your wardrobe. Take a look at your closet. Do you have multiple sizes in your closet? Would you have more clothes to wear if you lost weight? Of course, weight is like debt—easy to put on and hard to take off.

Would going to the gym be a better use of your time rather than buying a whole new wardrobe to fit your new dimensions? Or maybe your new weight is the real one, and you should sell your too-small clothes at a consignment store to make money to buy the replacement items.

Buy pre-used and trendy

Young people are adopting the trend for "gently pre-worn" clothes, too. For example, Heidi's sons take their clothes to a Buffalo Exchange store and trade them in for things they like even more. When you shop at any of these kinds of consignment or thrift stores, make friends with the store personnel and volunteers. They can help you find what you are looking for. These places scrimp on prices and they scrimp on dressing rooms, so wear form-fitting clothes you can try clothes on over.

You will be pleasantly surprised to find that many of these stores accept only currently trendy, brand-name items. They have spawned the term "trashion," or fashion made from recycled items. An Eco-Couture Fashion Show was held in Long Beach a few years ago with styles created from clothes purchased at Goodwill www.ShopGoodwill.com stores. Salvation Army www.SalvationArmyUSA.org is called "Sallies" by frugalista fans. Even Hollywood celebrities can get frugal fever. For example, Angelina Jolie got into the act a few years ago when she wore a crushed black velvet gown on the red carpet. It was purchased at Wasteland, www.Wasteland.com located on avant-garde Melrose Avenue in Los Angeles. The cost? It was $26. An added benefit for environmentally minded: recycled merchandise is better than buying new. The concept is to reduce, reuse, and recycle. Reduce by giving clothes you do not need to others. Reuse by buying other people's clothes. Recycle by giving old things new purpose.

Online clothes shopping

Online clothes shopping works if you can guesstimate your correct size. The web is a good place for plus-size clothes, extra wide or extra-narrow shoes, and other uncommon sizing needs. www.CouponCabin.com has clothing coupons for major retailers online. Look for double and triple-coupon deals and put all your coupons in your coupon organizer.

Online designer consignment stores are abound in this economy. Here are a few: www.MySistersCloset.com, A Red Carpet Life at www.stores.ebay.com.my/A-Red-Carpet-Life, Decades Two at www.stores.ebay.com/DecadesTwo, and Mama Stone Vintage at www.stores.ebay.com/mama-stone-vintage.

Choose items that are EUC for "excellent used condition" and sellers with ratings of at 98 percent or higher. Pay with a credit card, not a debit card so you have purchase protection. If you like trolling through vintage shops online, you can indulge yourself at deep discounts here: www.RentTheRunway.

com, www.JitterBuzz.com, www.RodeoDriveSale.com, www. ArchiveVintage.com, www.Vintage70sClothing.com, www. FemminasStyle.com, www.SwankVintage.com, and Red Rose Vintage Clothing at www.rrnspace.com.

Online accessories shopping

Accessories create the look you want. If you want to rent designer accessories (or make some money renting out your own designer merchandise), go to www.avelle.com (formerly www.BagBorroworSteal.com). You can rent luxury brand earrings, totes, or watches at a monthly or weekly rate for a $60 annual fee. Think of it as a Netflix for accessories. If you want to get cash for your gently-used designer handbags, accessories, and jewelry, check out www.JillsConsignment.com.

If you are a shoe fan, you may know that www.zappos.com offers free standard shipping both ways. If you love jewelry, you can flash some gorgeous gems that do not require insurance. Check out very realistic-looking cubic zirconium from www. MystiqueGems.com and other costume jewelers. You can make money selling your unworn fine jewelry, diamonds, and watches to Circa, www.CircaJewels.com. You can take an old gold piece to your jeweler to have it melted down and restyled into a new design.

Luxury accessories online

Several sites help designers unload returns and excess inventory without losing their elite status. Some of these sites attempt to create an allure of exclusivity by being "invitation only." It is necessarily difficult to get an invitation. For example, if you are a www.MORE.com magazine reader, you can go to www.gilt.com/more to sign up. Other online guides and outlets include www.ShipItToMe.com, www.DealDivine.com, www. TopButton.com, and www.6pm.com.

Deals on designer clothes, shoes, and accessories can be found online at www.BlueFly.com, www.RueLaLa.com, www.

HauteLook.com, www.Ideeli.com, www.Gilt.com, www.Net-a-Porter.com, and www.TheOutlet.com.

You also can rent designer fashions online at www.RentTheRunway.com and www.WearTodayGoneTomorrow.com. Rentals run from $50 to $200 for a several-night loan, and they are shipped to your door. If you can part with several of your designer handbags, some sites resell them on consignment, taking a 30 percent consignment fee. Upload a few digital photos, get approval, and then ship the bag to the online services which will inspect the bag, confirm its authenticity, and give you a quote. You then sign a consignment contract and the bag goes online. When it is sold, you get a check in the mail.

If you are a handbag fanatic, here are some online handbag consignment stores: www.Fashionphile.com, www.YoogisCloset.com, www.StrictlyPursonal.com, and www.CovetShop.com.

Each of these sites receives more than a hundred bags a week for consideration. Perhaps the days of handbag insanity are becoming "so yesterday." At least there is a trend for logos to be more subtle, as seen in Louis Vuitton's recent line of logo-less handbags.

Know that you are not alone

A recent study claims that three in four wealthy women say they will buy a luxury item only if they perceive that it is "a good deal." They are reportedly looking for classic styles that will last more than one season. The trend in luxury goods is value in the form of quality and staying power.

"I think the critical metric here is the balance between price and value," reports a design house president. Donna Karan admitted, "I don't think we've looked at real clothes for a long time, so it's sort of like a new reality." Another designer claimed, "I'm ready for real clothes, things that I want to buy and keep for years." With recessionary times, the new status symbol has become spending well, not spending mindlessly. Sam, who buys his shirts and suits at fine stores only when they are on sale, is example of just such a consumer.

One recession-driven trend is luxury makers providing "bridge" (lower priced) lines. For example, Manolo Blahnik and Coach came out with new collections at lower price points. Another trend is tying purchases to donations to social causes.

Another recession-driven trend is clothes you can wear right away. Heidi started reporting about the fashion industry in the 1980s and had to "wrap her mind around" the ingrained practice in retail to stock clothes ahead of the season. That means bikinis in late winter and coats in late summer. The idea never made much sense to her. Upscale designer Elie Tahari recently said that most of the clothes he is shipping can be worn right away. "The consumer has a lot more savvy and smarts. She is buying what she needs, and she's wearing it right away." Buy what you need and nothing more.

REAL LIFE CASE STUDY
"A Reader's Tips and YouTube Video"
Written by *TheSmartestWay*™ fan Jin Rong

1. *Lower the water heater temperature.*

2. *Unplug unused or seldom used electronics or appliances.*

3. *Adjust tax withholdings to have a bigger paycheck to invest or pay off debts. Why give the government a free loan in which they pay you back your own money the next year?*

4. *Make donations of unused items.*

5. Turn off computer monitors, or at least use screensaver and PC hibernation settings.

6. If you are very disciplined, use a credit card to get cash back. Typical returns are 1-2 percent (depending on the card type).

7. Cook your own meals instead of eating out so often.

8. Do not fall for gimmick 3D or IMAX movies.

9. Remove heavy/useless items in the car. Don't forget, additional weight contributes to gas usage.

10. Exercise!!! That's the best way to save money, not have any health problems. Medical costs are skyrocketing each year.

11. Use coupons to save.

12. Eliminate collision coverage from auto insurance if your vehicle is worth less than $5,000. Typically, you save $300/yr.

13. Grow your own food. It's healthier and organic. But make sure the cost of building and maintaining the garden is not higher than buying the food itself.

14. Turn off lights when not in use or get lower wattage bulbs.

15. Go for a longer hairstyle so you frequent the barber less often.

16. *Get rid of unnecessary luxuries such as digital cable or additional packages, data plan for Smart phones, or super-fast internet cable plans.*

Chapter 11

SAVE ON HOW TO BUY CLOTHES

"When reason rules, money is a blessing."
—Publilius Syrus

IN OUR FIRST BOOK, Heidi explained her shopping technique in what she called the Ten Question Test. Here is the expanded version. Whenever Heidi finds an item she might like, she puts it through the Ten Question Test. Everyone has purchased something that they thought they needed at the time, only to bring it home and find that they don't use it. This test is the secret to making sure you are spending your hard-earned dollars on things you really want and need. How about writing these 10 questions on an index card, storing it in your wallet, and reading when you go shopping?

1. **Do I really need this item?** Has this ever happened to you? You see a garment in a store and think, "I really need that." You bring it home and find that you already have something similar in your closet. We all know the clothes we like, and it is tempting to just keep buying more of them.

2. **Would I wear it often?** You may believe you need the item, but how often will you wear it? Can you "dress it up or dress it down"? Suppose you want a black sweater. Note that not all black sweaters are made alike. Often, even in the same store, you can find a better black sweater at a lower price. It just takes some searching. For example, if you think you need an evening gown, ask yourself how often you attend charity balls or elegant weddings. Attempt versatility. If you had a dressy top and skirt instead of one gown, could you wear the dressy top with jeans for going out to the movies? How versatile is it? Can you wear this black sweater both for work and casual or work and evening? You need clothes to do "double duty" and work hard for you. Would you wear it in different kinds of weather? Will it span some seasonal changes, or would you wear this only a few times a year? Is it limited in its application? It's not as good an investment if it is so "fashionable" that you will only wear it one season.

3. **Does it coordinate well with outfits that I already own?** You are trying to put together clothes that play well together and don't fight. This is not the time to introduce an item to your closet that is too bright or too dull, or too flashy or too conservative for your other clothes. If this item is a color or style that doesn't "go with" anything else you own, you shouldn't buy it no matter how "fun" or "different" it may seem. Heidi's Mom has a saying, "Variety is the spice of life." If it's a trendy, new color for your wardrobe, make sure that it coordinates with the neutrals in your wardrobe. Neutrals are the blacks, tans, grays, and navies that you already have. If not, the item will sit in your closet, scolding you until you go out and buy other things that coordinate with it. You don't need that hassle. Also, ask

yourself which accessories—shoes, belts, handbags, etc.—will coordinate with this new item. A good shoe repair shop can dye your handbag or shoes to match an outfit or each other. By the way, shoe repair shops are a good place to find quality handbags, belts, and luggage. Heidi has found some of her favorite pieces there.

4. **Does it fit the image I'm trying to present?** What is your image? Eclectic isn't the right answer for a versatile, economized wardrobe. Your work wardrobe should receive the bulk of your wardrobe budget. What does your boss and your boss's boss wear? You don't want to be considered "too lightweight" at work and be overlooked for a promotion because you don't dress like the position you deserve. Your closet should embody your own personal "work" look, as well as your own personal "casual" look. Classic shapes and neutral colors are best for your career basics—pants, skirts, and jackets. They will carry you through each season for years to come. After you collect the basics in black and neutrals, then add your personality with a coordinated accent color and updated shirts and accessories.

5. **Is it priced well for the value?** If you're convinced you need it, the tricky part is to determine price versus value. First, determine how much value the item holds for you. Try not to buy anything that is not on sale. We recommend not buying non-necessities unless they are at least 50 percent off the original price.

6. **Is it made well enough so I can wear it over several years?** If you like an item, you'll want to wear it for more than a few months. Unfortunately, it's difficult to determine how well an item will "wear." A single laundering could make it look like it's ready to

be donated to a thrift shop. Some items will launder well and look like new for years. Avoid items that already look shabby or wrinkled in the store, unless shabby and wrinkled is the look you're seeking. Also, consider the cost of dry cleaning. Will you be able to hang out the wrinkles in a steamed-up bathroom, or will you be paying for the garment many times over with your dry cleaning bill? If it will require ironing, do you really have the time to iron? Heidi has several times found out she can hand wash dry-cleanable items, but it is always a risk. You never know how an item will respond to washing and wearing, so make your best guess. Men's dress shirts can be laundered at home and then just pressed at the dry cleaners. Men's neckties often double as napkins, unfortunately. A proactive spray of fabric protector can help remove inevitable stains. Stains are the best reason to not overspend on ties. If an item needs alterations, your tailor can shorten pants and skirts and make the shoulders narrower. They can nip in the waist. If it is too long, or snug, check the inner seams to see if seams are wide and can be let out.

7. Would I want to wear it for several years? Assuming the garment is well made and will wear well, you will have it in your closet for years to come. Will you want to wear it for years to come? Is the style timeless enough that you can see yourself wearing it even though trends change, which they inevitably will? Is it so trendy that you'll be bored with it soon? Will it be cast off as "so last season" before you know it? The price has to be amazingly low if it's a short-term, trendy piece. Look for garments that are so classic that you can use them as the foundation of your personal style. Classic styles come in and out of fashion regularly. Sheath dresses, cardigan sweaters, and turtleneck sweaters always are "au current" for women. Mock turtlenecks, pullover t-shirts, and sweaters under a tweed blazer always look good on men, year after year. Both men and women can be chic in chinos, denim jackets, and black leather bomber jackets no matter the current trends.

8. **Can I afford the expense right now?** This is a question you can answer only by being honest with yourself. Consider the other non-necessity expenses you've allowed yourself already this month. Consider the events, gifts, or projects that you're saving up for. Try to balance how much you want this item, compared to how much you want the other expenses in your life right now. Just because you have money in your pocket or your checking account doesn't mean you should be buying it right now. On the other hand, if you came to the store specifically to buy a black sweater at this price, that's different.

9. **Does it fit perfectly?** Only after the item passes the first eight questions does Heidi place it in her cart. She'll try on the items in the cart if she has the time and the energy to try them on. Sad, but true, items that look great on the hanger may look not-so-great on the body, and vice versa. Do not skip the crucial step of "trying before buying." Find a good, reasonably priced tailor, perhaps at your dry cleaners. Know what can and cannot be altered successfully. Generally, garments can be shortened in hems and sleeves, and shoulders and hips can be narrowed. To let things out after you have gained is more difficult, since seam allowances may be too narrow, and exposed seams may still show. As Heidi learned in journalism school, "When in doubt, keep it out." If you find yourself having too many concerns, do not buy it.

10. **Would I regret it if I don't buy it?** When all the other questions earn a "yes" answer, this is the final question. Usually there is a voice inside you that says either, "I would like to have it, but I can surely live without it," or "I would always remember that I let this one get away." Does the item meet the other nine criteria above? Is it so perfect and so well-priced that you would "kick yourself" for not getting it? If so, then, and only then, put it in the cart and take it to the dressing room for the all-important fit-and-mirror test. If you try it on and it fits, put it on hold and go do another errand for a "cooling off period." If the items is still saying "buy me!" in your mind later, perhaps it's time to head back to the store and stand in the checkout line.

Know when to shop and who to shop with

Weekdays are less hectic than weekends, and you will get better service from the sales staff. Research the stores where you will be shopping. Shop seasonally and plan ahead. The best bargains are at the end of the season when stores need to get rid of prior inventory before bringing in new things. For instance, when the store wants to bring in the bikinis, they have sales on their winter jackets. Wait until after the back-to-school rush ends before you buy your kids their school clothes. Each school has its own fashion trends. Wait until your kids check out what everyone is wearing first. Ask your friends to save their hand-me-downs and swap with each other, or their friends.

Do not shop with a friend who is a shopaholic. Shop alone or with a friend who will tell you the truth about how the garment looks on you. Shop with a friend who cares about your finances and does not want you to overspend.

Heidi has this arrangement with her husband that saves them both a lot of money on their clothes. They help each other shop for clothes, and they will purchase only clothes that the other person thinks looks attractive and is well-priced.

Online shopping tips

Online shopping used to be almost entirely tax free. Recently, more states have started collecting sales tax on the sale of merchandise purchased online. For online sales, comparison shop and request alerts when your desired item goes on sale. You can avail yourself of the alert services at www.Find.com, www.PriceGrabber.com, www.shopzilla.com, www.ShopStyle. com, www.BensBargains.com, www.DealsOfAmerica.com, www.BuyBargainBuddy.com, and www.SlickDeals.net. Just be very, very careful that you don't get crazy "saving" on things you do not need!

High fashion for low prices can be found at www. PeoplesStyleWatch.com, www.InStyle.com, www.ShopThe Look.net, www.Endless.com, www.TheOutnet.com, and www. Bluefly.com.

To find an online auction item you want to bid on, be specific in your search by also typing size, brand, and color in the search box. Shop with sellers with at least a nine percent rating. Read descriptions carefully. "Resembles" or "looks like" are not the real deal. Note when the auction will end and come in as one of the last bidders.

Warning: These websites can become addictive. They are designed to develop cravings. Even the email alerts of a pending sale can become a "fix" in themselves. How exciting to be "in the know"! The array of "must-have merch" changes quickly, is deeply reduced, and is in limited quantities. There even is a ticking clock, a la television shopping networks, to lure you into saying "Yes!" before you come to your senses.

Online stores entice you to place items in your online shopping cart or on your "wish list." They email you friendly reminders about what you "forgot" to buy, or what you might wish to buy, or what "other people like you" did buy. Retailers are experts at impulse buying and social pressure psychology. Just so you know…

Calculate the shipping and handling costs, which you wouldn't pay if you bought the item at the store. If you might return the item, you may have to pay return shipping, too.

Whatever you do, do not let alcohol diminish your capacity to maintain your mental and financial stability. You do not want to become a BUI, Buyer Under the Influence. Sipping and shopping can become a very expensive habit. Deals and drinking do not mix. Friends do not let friends buy drunk. There are no online traffic police to pull you over and ask you if you know what you are doing. Nevertheless, there is danger. Online shopping binges can lead to financial hangovers. Alcohol doubles the headache and the amount of overspending. We recommend that you save that Cosmopolitan for after you have made your purchases sober.

More online shopping tips

In the thrill of the hunt, keep in mind some of the basic laws of pricing:

- A $3.99 item seems like a better deal than an item priced at $4.00.
- A $200 dress seems like a better deal when it is compared to a $400 dress.
- "Buy-one-get-one-free" is not a bargain when you would not normally buy one.
- Just because something is tagged with a high price does not mean it is worth the price.
- Just because something is deeply discounted does not mean it is now a bargain.

Use online coupons. Find the codes by searching online. In your search engine, type in the merchant's name and "promotion code" or "discount code." You can find coupons at www.CouponMoutain.com, www.CouponCabin.com, www.

DealCoupon.com, www.FatWallet.com, www.Ebates.com, www.FindSavings.com, and www.JumpOnDeals.com.

Place the items you want in your virtual shopping cart and then enter the coupon code when checking out. If your discount does not show up prior to submitting your order, the coupon code or link may have expired.

Like all coupons, watch out for small print that explains expiration dates and minimum purchases. You can set up email alerts so you can be notified of sales, but do this very selectively. If you are buying online, check out eBay's resources for frauds and scams on the site.

For security, remove your credit card information from your online account. You can usually do this by going into your account. The less personal information you leave on the Internet, the less vulnerable you are to cyber theft. Also, you will be less inclined to make quick purchases if you have to pull out your credit card and log in the number each time.

Watch out for add-on or up-sell offers that include a subscription to monthly deliveries of the product or a magazine subscription. You have a specified period in which to cancel the subscription, after which time you will be billed for the upcoming delivery. It's no surprise that most people forget to cancel.

Alternatives to shopping

You may like something, but you do not have to own it! Window shopping is a perfectly acceptable form of entertainment. You can spend an enjoyable afternoon at the mall with very little money. Tell yourself that you are perfectly capable of not buying everything you see that you like. You can browse from store to store with a friend, point out trends to each other, and have fun.

Here are some great, no-cost places to go window shopping: shop in your family's closet and your friends' closets! Some of Heidi's favorite shirts and jackets were pilfered from her husband's and her son's coat closet. She has petite girlfriends who find great deals in the children's section of the department store. Do you have a friend who wears the same size as you to borrow a few items from your closet and borrow a few things from hers, too? Also, try a clothing exchange party. It is like a cookie exchange, but less fattening. Ask your friends to bring the clothes they no longer want, pile them onto a table, and take whatever they want. Donate the remaining items to a thrift store. You can also try the "absence makes the heart grow fonder" technique. In the winter, put your warm weather clothes in another closet or store them under your bed. When winter is over, you will feel like you have a new wardrobe.

Going on a clothes diet

Ask yourself honestly if you truly have found every possible new outfit combination of your clothes? Do you really have to go out and buy more clothes? Or could you create some new looks with what you already own? The latest fashion trend is less matching and more unmatched. Isn't your wardrobe sufficient enough to quit clothes shopping for a week, a month, a year? If something is truly missing from your closet that you just can't survive without, what is it? If you need to replace a worn-out basic piece, such as nice black trousers, buy that item. Then stop shopping. Just stop! Believe it or not, there is more to life than shopping.

Clothes were Heidi's primary focus during her "fashion phase" when she was a student at The Fashion Institute of Design and Merchandising, when she was the news editor of Apparel News Group, and when she was a personal shopper at Nordstrom. Now she rarely shops for clothes. Why? Because she has "enough" (yes, it's possible.), and over the years, she has also developed a closet full of classic, hardworking clothes that are appropriate for any occasion. Some of her favorite pieces are more than 20 years old and still going strong. Some of the oldest pieces get the most compliments. Newer is not necessarily better.

Dr. April Benson promoted the clothes-diet concept based on her interview with the author of *My Year Without Clothes Shopping* by Jill Chivers, an Australian corporate facilitator. Chivers started a blog to keep her accountable to her decision to not buy clothes for a year. Her blog became so popular that it became a book. Then Chivers developed a year-long program for online subscribers who want to embark on a no-new-clothes adventure as she did.

Some people like to stop the shopping insanity and save their clothing funds for something more enduring than the latest fashion. Practicing the principle of being good global citizens, they buy less and donate more. There are community groups whose members have a pact among themselves to no longer buy things that are new, to buy only items that are pre-used and recycled. To encourage each other and a sense of community, they set up potluck dinners and clothes swapping parties.

We guarantee you that there are many productive, long-range uses for the money you will save by curbing, if not completely cutting, your clothing budget.

Other necessities of life

You will notice that this book does not address other necessities of life, such as gasoline, utility bills, and phone bills. Please read our first book, **TheSmartestWay™ to Save, Why You Can't Hang onto Money and What to Do About It,** for more information on these topics.

REAL LIFE CASE STUDY
"Teaching Kids the Importance of Saving Money"
Written by *TheSmartestWay*™ fan Bryan Carey
Owner of www.MoneySavingParent.com

Personal finance is a highly neglected subject, not just in schools, but in families as well. As parents, it is important to teach children the importance of saving money, and the first step is to start the education process early. The sooner children learn about saving money, the more likely they will be to continue this practice into adulthood.

One of the earliest and most popular options to introduce children to the concept of saving money is a piggy bank. I have two daughters and they each have their own piggy bank. These coin and cash receptacles are useful as an early means for financial education, and they come in many sizes, shapes, and styles. My girls opted for the simple variety, but there are many choices, and with minimal searching, parents can find one to fit their child's personality and interest. Some include sound effects, some count the money automatically, and others are created around a specific theme. Whatever suits your child's interests is fine. The investment in a piggy bank will easily pay off with the financial lessons it teaches.

Another savings vehicle that all parents should start for each child is an education savings account. It can be a Section 529, Coverdell Education Savings, or other investment. My girls each have an education savings account, and they enjoy reading their quarterly statements, asking questions about the balance, and watching as their savings accumulate. Thus, an education savings account serves two important purposes. It helps to pay for future college expenses, and it helps to teach children about the saving process and how it will improve their future.

Setting financial goals is another way I teach my kids about money. If there is something they want, I establish a savings goal with them and challenge them to save the necessary *funds until they have enough cash to make the purchase. As an added incentive, I will often agree to match their savings efforts, dollar for dollar. I will reward them with money when they complete homework, help with household chores, etc. They can spend the money if they like, or they can opt to drop the cash into their piggy bank. If they decide on the latter, I will match the money.*

Last, and most important of all, I teach my girls by setting an example. It would make no sense to talk about the importance of saving money if I was spending frivolously and never setting aside any money for the future. My wife and I operate the web site www.moneysavingparent.com, and we strive not only to educate other parents about money, but also to save our own money whenever possible. The example we set proves, to our girls, that saving money isn't just something to talk about or something that only matters when you are young. Saving money needs to be a lifetime discipline, and it is something we practice and strive to improve on a regular basis.

TheSmartestWay™
TO SAVE —
ON YOUR "WANTS"

Chapter 12

SAVING AT RESTAURANTS

*"Good thoughts are no better than good dreams,
unless they be executed."*

—Ralph Waldo Emerson

EVER SINCE she was a little girl, Heidi has loved eating at restaurants. What a pleasure to sit down, select from a menu, and have someone deliver exactly what you ordered, and no dishes to wash afterward! Since she is not fond of cooking, restaurants are a special treat.

So, how do you indulge your desire to not cook, and still not literally eat your savings account?

Find restaurant coupons

You can find restaurant coupons from www.Restaurant.com, www.restaurants.com, www.DinnerBroker.com, and www. OpenTable.com, and many other websites. For example, www. Restaurants.com sells discount restaurant certificates. Here is how the site works. You enter your zip code to find the participating restaurants that will sell certificates at a discount. On the first day of the month, a $25 certificate will cost $10 and even less a few weeks later. You may only use one certificate per month per restaurant.

You also will find restaurant coupons in your local newspapers, mailers, and flyers. Coupons for restaurants are the way to go. Entertainment coupon books are okay if you know you will use enough of the coupons to cover your cost for the book. Heidi bought one of those books one time and found that she didn't use enough coupons before they expired. On the other hand, Sam bought one when he was newly married and used a two-for-one coupon that saved him the cost of the coupon book in one meal. Coupon sites are like one happy family. For example, if you go to a site by visiting www.CouponMom.com first, you save an additional percentage on your order. If you register with that site, you can get a 40 percent discount on the www.Restaurant.com. This is "affiliate marketing" at work. Find other coupons by typing in your search engine browser: restaurant, coupon, and the name of your city.

Use restaurant coupons

To get feedback on discount codes, check out the feedback on www.RetailMeNot.com. Even airlines are getting into the act by allowing you to trade in your miles for restaurant certificates. Yes, you can use coupons and certificates together. Before you book your reservation, double check any restrictions on black-out dates and minimum purchase requirements. At the restaurant, when you are ordering, discreetly mention the coupons to the waiter.

Restaurants such as Chevy's Mexican restaurant www.chevys.com will give you a payment receipt with information about how to earn a coupon. You go online, input the code on the receipt, and fill out a survey. Then you will receive an email coupon for a discount on your next visit to the restaurant. This provides the restaurant valuable feedback and incentivizes you to return to that restaurant. You can sign up for El Torito www.eltorito.com, Chili's www.chilis.com, and Buca di Beppo www.bucadibeppo.com and they will send you weekly coupons. This is a growing trend, so ask your favorite restaurant.

Heidi and her husband keep restaurant coupons in an envelope in the car. When they are out on the road and need to go to a restaurant, they look through their restaurant coupon envelope. On the other hand, they don't let the fact that they have a coupon determine how often they dine at restaurants. For example, they don't think, "We have a coupon; therefore, we should go out to eat tonight." In other words, the situation dictates the coupon; the coupon doesn't dictate the situation.

Avoid expensive fast food

Drive-through restaurants and vending machines can really carve into your food budget. To handle hunger pangs quickly and inexpensively, Heidi packs her own snack bag. She keeps a small plastic bag in the refrigerator that holds snacks such as string cheese, nuts, raisins, apple slices, bananas, granola bars, chips, crackers, pretzels, or cookies. She grabs it and puts it into her tote whenever she is out on meetings and might be tempted by overpriced, overprocessed fast food. When her children were young, having snacks on hand was a must. If you end up buying fast food, buy something healthy, such as chicken at El Polo Loco, www.ElPolloLoco.com, a salad at Wendy's www.Wendys.com or McDonald's www.McDonalds.com, a grilled chicken sandwich at Burger King www.BK.com, or a salad or sandwich at Subway www.Subway.com. If your refrigerator, freezer, and pantry are sufficiently stocked, you can avoid last-minute trips to the drive-through or an emergency call for pizza delivery. Figure out how to eliminate those wallet sappers, such as coffee shops, vending machines, concession stands, and the candy display at check-out counters. Keep plenty of bottled water in your car.

Know which are the best restaurants

For high-end restaurants, book your reservation online with www.OpenTable.com or www.DinnerBroker.com to earn reward points. You earn even more points if your reservation time is a little early or late. For trendy, low-end dining, there is gourmet street food. One of these mobile eateries may be headed for your town. Confirmed foodies can sign up to be a mystery shopper. You start with fast food assignments and eventually the more upscale eateries, such as Ruth's Chris Steakhouse and Fleming's Prime Steakhouse. A list of companies for mystery shopping is on www.FreelanceByU.com under the link to "working at home" on the left column.

For meeting with clients, eating on the job is taking on a new twist. Expensive power lunches are out of vogue. Creativity is in style. Bookstores and museums have classy cafes to meet for a cup of coffee. Clients and prospects will appreciate your underlying message of financial responsibility.

Sign up for the birthday club at your favorite restaurants, and they will email you a coupon to use near your birthday time, as well as coupons throughout the year. Buca di Beppo www.bucadibeppo.com has a birthday club. If you have children, they can eat free at Denny's www.dennys.com, Chevy's www.chevys.com, and other restaurants on certain nights. Find out more at www.KidsEatFree.com. Ask your favorite restaurants if they have an "early-bird" special. You can find an up-to-date list of restaurants that offer birthday clubs and discounts at www.freebiesandmuchmore.com.

More restaurant tips

Go on special discount or family days. Patronize restaurants that offer menus that have more reasonably priced entrees and two-for-one deals such as T.G.I. Friday's www.Fridays.com and Ruby Tuesday www.rubytuesday.com. Look for new restaurants offering opening specials to attract customers. Explore new kinds of food, including lower priced, healthier ethnic cuisines. At food courts, try the free samples so you won't need to buy as much for lunch.

If you like an elegant restaurant once in a while, do not despair. Rediscover restaurant bars. Steakhouse chains such as Morton's Steakhouse www.Mortons.com have $5 food and $4 drinks at the bar. Flemings Steakhouse www. FlemingsSteakHouse.com has $6 appetizers (including ravioli, calamari, and a prime cheese and bacon burger) served at the happy hour in the bar until 7 p.m. There are many websites that will provide coupons for fine dining, including Ruth's Chris Steakhouse www.RuthsChris.com. Just type in your favorite restaurant and the word coupon! Results will pop up from www.CouponCodeSaving.com, www.Mahalo.com, www. CardPool.com, www.ChowHound.com, www.DealNews.com, and many others.

Make your waiter your friend so you can avoid extra charges. Ask if they will provide bread and water for your table (meaning you do not intend to pay for it.) "May we have some tap water, please?" "Is bread included with that?" If you want to split your meal, make sure there is no charge for an extra plate.

Know what to do at a restaurant

If you can have a light snack before you leave for the restaurant, you will not be so hungry by the time the waiter takes your order. Lunch specials are less expensive than regular lunch. Lunch is less expensive than dinner. Appetizers and sides are less expensive than entrees. Happy hours usually last more than an hour on weeknights. Heidi's favorite happy hour is held twice each weeknight, about four to six and then nine to closing. Happy hours have good deals on appetizers or free appetizers. The reason is simple. They want you to order more overpriced drinks. Just order your one drink and eat heartily. Pay for each drink with cash and do not start a bar tab, for obvious reasons. When Heidi is handed a menu, she scans the entire list to find the appetizers, vegetable sides, and the soup of the day.

Some restaurants add a "split charge" or "extra plate" fee. Ask if there is one. She and her husband have been splitting an entrée or dessert at restaurants for years. Lately, their friends have been doing it, too. One person can order an entrée and the other person can order a bowl of soup or a side salad. There is no stigma, especially in these days of dieting and conserving resources. A group of friends can enjoy ordering a couple of desserts and everyone taking a few bites from each plate. Tapas-like small plates and a trio of mini-burgers called sliders are perfectly acceptable items to order. Sharing a plate of food is no longer considered taboo. Casual restaurants are embracing this trend with value-priced items to be passed around the table. Following the example of Cheesecake Factory, California Pizza Kitchen recently created a "small cravings" menu.

Beverages cost way too much. Tap water with lemon is healthier, has fewer calories, and allows you to taste your food. Waiters like to suggest bottled water because it has a huge mark-up. They may "turn up their nose" when you indicated that tap water is good enough for you. Their job is to increase your bill, which will increase their tip. Nevertheless, bottled water is overpriced, overhyped, and may not be any purer than your city's own. If you order a drink, such as iced tea, request "easy on the ice." Another hype is high prices for organic dishes. If you like wine with dinner, find out if the restaurant charges a "corkage fee." This is a fee restaurants charge to open the cork of your own bottle if you bring your own. Sometimes the price of a decent bottle of wine from the store is the same price as a single glass of wine at a restaurant. Some restaurants will waive your corkage fee on slow nights, such as Sundays and Mondays.

Desserts are also overpriced. An alternative is to go out for frozen yogurt or ice cream after dinner, or buy a pint of gourmet ice cream on sale at the store, go home, and dig in. If you have only appetizers or sides at the restaurant, you could splurge on dessert, or skip everything but dessert. You can go out for just dessert, later in the evening, say after a movie. Eating less is good for both your wallet and your waistline.

Doggy-bag it

"Waste not; want not." This was ingrained in Heidi's consciousness by her Mom. To this day, she can't bear to see perfectly edible food scraped off dinner plates into trash barrels. When you throw away food, you throw away money. If you care about the environment, you could make a case that throwing away food also hurts the environment, because you are requiring all the resources to make additional food to replace what was thrown out. Food, one of the basic elements of life, is a terrible thing to waste.

This is especially true at restaurants. For heaven's sake, take home a doggy bag, even if you do not own a dog! Many foods taste even better the next day, especially pasta dishes. If you order a salad, ask for the dressing on the side and dress only the half portion you're going to eat at the restaurant. Sam is a consummate doggy bagger. He even asks for the contents of the bread basket to be put in the bag, if he likes the bread. You can slice the bread, add some cheese and mustard and mayo, and make a sandwich to take to the office the next day. For decades, at restaurants, Heidi's husband has eaten only half of what is on his plate. The rest goes home in a doggie bag for another meal later. He has a trim waistline as an added benefit. Once he apologized to one of his clients after lunch, and the client mentioned that when he has lunch with a billionaire friend of his, "she always takes a doggie bag home."

REAL LIFE CASE STUDY
"A Bright Future in Difficult Times"
Written by *TheSmartestWay*™ fan Steve Staten

While attending college full time, I worked 20 hours a week and saved to buy my first car. It took me over three months of searching every day to find the car I wanted at the price

I wanted to pay. I saved about $2,000 under the Kelly Blue Book value by being patient and doing my research. I bought almost everything used on sites like Craigslist or eBay. I can honestly say almost none of the used items I bought were noticeably used, damaged, or broken, and all lasted as long as new items. After graduating, I continued with the job I had in college, and I am now working full time. I was unable to find a more career-oriented job due to the down economy. In order to save money, I moved back home with my parents, after four years away, and built up an emergency fund.

Just recently, I landed a new job. Despite the fact that I am making more money, I continue to live at home. I have been putting all the additional income toward the remainder of my student loans. They are all on automatic withdrawal, way above the minimums. Since I'm living on about the same amount of money I did in college, I don't even miss the 'extra' money. It just comes right out of my paycheck. I am also saving towards a down payment for my first house, which will be a multi-unit income property. I'm planning to live in one of those units to save money and help pay down my mortgage faster.

I've set up a great budget using the principals in your first book **TheSmartestWay™ to Save, Why You Can't Hang onto Money and What to Do About It** and through www.Mint.com, and I've got a number of financial goals, with realistic timelines. Just last week, I attended the annual shareholders meeting for my credit union and was elected to the Board of Directors; at 25 years old, I'm the youngest person ever to serve on the board. I'm excited for the experience and financial lessons I will learn through that new commitment as well.

Chapter 13

SAVING ON OTHER ITEMS

*"If you buy things you don't need,
you are stealing from yourself."*
—Czechoslovakian Proverb

OW MUCH are you spending on the things you want, but don't need? Try to never pay retail again, on anything! There are so many places to get what you want at a discount. Tell yourself, "If it is not on sale, it does not exist." If you see something you want that isn't on sale, it probably will be on sale next week. Save your receipts for two weeks, then contact the store to see if your item has gone on sale. If so, the store may give you the difference in cash.

Before you shop, look at www.ConsumerReports.com to find out the best brands and models. You can buy stamps at a discount at www.usps.com, www.eBay.com, www.stamps.com, and www.endicia.com.

You can save by ordering your eyeglasses online at www. EyeBuyDirect.com and other sites. They even allow you to upload a photo of yourself on the site and then "try on" the frames virtually. This will show you how the frames will look on you, but not how they will feel. Nevertheless, the savings may make it worthwhile.

If you are an avid reader and buy a lot of books, the prices of Kindles, Nooks, and other electronic readers are dropping. The lower prices of electronic books could save you the one-time cost of the electronic reader.

Get things for free

A favorite source of all things free online is at www. FreeCycle.com. Offline, all sorts of merchandise, books, and appliances are available for free. In some cases, you may have to fill out a detailed questionnaire or make a little bit of effort to find them. In other cases, you have to buy something to get something free, especially on websites such as www.Walmart. com and www.Sephora.com. These are incentives to pry your credit card number from you. The power of the magical word F-R-E-E is stronger than you may realize. Make sure you are not spending extra money just to "save" money by getting "free" stuff.

The Suggested Reading list at the back of the book has many books on free things and good deals. One free thing we can enjoy in America is tap water. Bottled water often is not any purer than what you can get from your own faucet. You can buy an inexpensive water filter, such as Brita or PUR, if you feel you need it. In any case, you do not need to pay for bottled water. You can pour your own water into a safely reusable metal or glass bottle that you can sterilize in the dishwasher. Help save the environment by not adding to the two million tons of plastic water bottles that are sent to landfills every year.

You can customize your own online radio station for free at www.Slacker.com and www.Pandora.com. You can get free shipping from many sites, including www.FreeShiping.org and www.FreeShippingOn.com. Try out a free budget management service at www.wesable.com. Free phone service through your computer is available at www.skype.com. You can get free Internet service at www.NetZero.com and free email accounts at Gmail.com, Hotmail.com and yahoo.com. Obtain a copy of your credit report at www.AnnualCreditReport.com. Free software downloads called "shareware" are available at sites such as www.Shutterfly.com, www.SnapFish.com, www. Flickr.com, and www.MindMeister.com.

Information abounds online. If you want to improve your home, check out www.DIY.com, www.HGTV.com, www. HomeDepot.com, www.Lowes.com, and www.ThisOldHouse. com.

You can also do a Google search for videos and instructions. Legal advice that may at least head you in the right direction can be found on such sites as www.nolo.com. Find out where you can surf the Internet for free at www.Wi-Fi-FreeSpotDirectory. com. Heidi likes the free photo-editing software www.Picasa. com. If you want to learn how to be more frugal, we suggest our own website, www.TheSmartestWay.com, as well as www. WiseBread.com, www.FrugalLiving.About.com, and www. FrugalDad.com among a host of other sites.

The U.S. Government Publication Office has free brochures on almost every topic. You can get free book downloads at www.Gutenberg.org. Wherever you see free samples, take some. You can get free boxes and envelopes sent to you with no shipping charge from the post office. Your doctor may be able to provide free sample medications, your dermatologist may have free skincare samples, and your dentist will probably be glad to give you free tooth brushes or dental floss. Shop at stores that give free samples, such as Costco.

Some free things require modest shipping charges. Beware of items that are "free" where shipping and handling charges are greater than the value of the item itself. Don't fall for those come-ons. Find out when they're going to be giving out samples in the grocery stores.

Save on electronics

You can even shop online while at a store. Some smart phones can scan the barcode label on an item and check the prices at other stores. Look for free apps such as ShopSavvy, Where to Shop, and Holiday Gift Guide, and apps by www. milo.com and www.amazon.com. Walmart will not match a price show on the screen of a phone, but Best Buy says it will. Whenever you buy anything, ask about the return policy. Whenever possible, get it in writing. When you purchase an item with a warranty, complete and return the warranty cards as soon as possible.

Here are some ways to keep your costs down on technology: www.PriceGrabber.com or www.PriceSpider.com for no charge will track prices and alert you if a product you're watching drops in price. At www.PriceProtector.com, you can sign up to receive an email alert if the price if an item you just bought is reduced. Ask the retailer you are buying from if they have a price-protection policy. If the price drops within 30 days of your purchase, they will credit or refund the difference. Consider electronics and appliances that are "factory refurbished."

What is to become of the millions of outdated, no-longer-wanted electronic devices? The garbage dumps don't want them, but people on the website www.sellingbin.com do. The site is not limited to electronics. If you want to get rid of your cell phone, sites such as www.PaceButler.com may pay you for it. Before buying a high-priced item, research it online, in Consumer Reports, and comparison shop. When buying small items, test them before leaving the store. Always ask about the return policy.

Think "dilute" and "combine"

You will be surprised how many things you can dilute with water. If it is liquid, consider the possibilities. This applies to cleaning products such as window cleaner and liquid hand soap. You can also dilute grooming products, such as shampoo, conditioner, and liquid hair spray. When bottles of lotion, bath gel, shampoo, and conditioner are empty, turn them upside down and drain out the very last drops. Do the same for bottles of dish soap, detergent, and liquid hand soap. Then add some water and swish to get that last application.

Diluting can also be used with beverages, such as diluting juices with water. Most juices are too sweet, especially for children. You can combine juices with each other to make a new flavor. You can combine leftover bottles of wine to make your own custom blend. Vintners do it all the time. They give blends the fancy name of "varietals." Coffee baristas do it, too. Try your own combinations of coffees and teas from whatever you have on hand.

When it comes to makeup, think about combining colors like an artist with a color palate. Heidi combines everything to get just the right color, including lipsticks, lip glosses, blushes, eye shadows, face powders, and nail polishes. A celebrity makeup artist she knows routinely blends custom shades on the inside of her arm. Heidi even combines her perfumes to make a signature scent. Her motto is, "use what you have to its best effect."

Rethink your grooming needs

Personal grooming is just that, personal. Some grooming products are perfect and cannot be replaced. Others deserve a second look, especially the very expensive products. Heidi shops for hair care products at Sally Beauty Supply stores www.SallyBeauty.com. The products are specifically for cosmetologists, but the store is open to the public.

It has been said that a woman's hair is her "crowning glory." Whether that is true or not, what is true is that women spend a tremendous amount of money at beauty salons. Many women of a "certain age" color their hair. Some women, however, look quite lovely with salt-and-pepper or silver hair. You should also consider your hairstyle. How much time and money does it require? Heidi has found that longer hair requires fewer appointments at the hair salon and less time to curl. She finally got the courage to ask her hairdresser to keep her appointments at a level, average price and her hairdresser agreed.

For manicures, shorter nails mean fewer appointments at the nail salon. You can save money on your manicures by asking the manicurist to trim your nails as short as possible. If you add acrylic nails, ask for a sheer pink color and no white French tips. That way, you have the option of painting them yourself if you want, between visits. At many hair and nail salons, cash is queen. Ask for a discount for paying in cash.

Heidi orders many Avon makeup and cosmetic products, a few of the perfumes, and even some of the handbags and jewelry. Her faithful Avon lady knows to expect emails from her inquiring about the sale prices. Heidi buys some of her lipsticks, eye shadows, and perfumes from dollar stores.

Rethink your exercise work-out needs

As far as keeping yourself in shape, if you are not using your gym membership, cancel it and save the money. You can borrow workout videos from the library. The Internet is full of customized exercise workouts, such as on the American Medical Association website www.ama-assn.org/go/health and www.cdc.gov/physicalactivity. Check out your local college or university for low-cost access to the pool and weight room. You can buy sports equipment and workout clothes on sale at discount stores such as Kmart and Target.

If you need a bicycle, one of the best places to shop is online police auctions. Police departments have warehouses full of property they have seized from thieves, everything from things with wheels, such as cars, motorcycles, bicycles, and wheelchairs, to the finer things in life, such as jewelry, computers, televisions, cameras, and stereos. As a manager of such a warehouse said, "Two things I've learned in this business. One: People will steal anything. Two: people will buy anything." In Los Angeles, the auction Is at www.PropertyRoom.com, and they have repossessed bikes galore.

Use the library

Our first book mentioned that libraries are a good source for borrowing books, tapes, DVDs, and books on tape or CD, as well as researching on the Internet for free. They also often have resources for learning a foreign language. Libraries are an excellent source for savings on entertainment and other areas. Many libraries have departments where they loan out art to decorate your home. When Heidi was in college, she decorated her apartment with a rotating exhibit of the old masters on loan from the library! Libraries also sponsor lectures, seminars, and movie nights at no or nominal cost. Sam's local library also has concerts and recitals that are free to the public.

One of Sam's fondest childhood memories is of the "Story Hour" every Saturday at his local library where he learned his love of books and reading. He remembers it as being more fun than going to the movies or other paid entertainments. Heidi took her own two sons every week to the library story hour for many years. They enjoyed the historic Pasadena Central Library. Check with the libraries in your area for dates and times. If they do not have a story hour, volunteer to help start one! Also, libraries can list job opportunities and provide you free access to computers and the Internet.

Do not fall for retailers' tricks

Retailers want you to buy impulsively, which should be no surprise to you! What may surprise you is how many ways retailers manage to manipulate shoppers. If you saw the movie, Minority Report, you may remember the scene in the mall in which the storefronts themselves spoke directly to Tom Cruise. They knew his buying preferences. Fiction became reality in 2011 when two malls set up a system to track shoppers' movements throughout the mall by monitoring the signals from their cell phones. The strategy was suspended when the U.S.

Senate intervened. Stores have other ways to influence your shopping. Here are some of the techniques used to increase their bottom line:

Stores are designed to encourage you to browse and linger. The music, scents, colors, and layouts of the store are the result of careful research. Here is how to fight back: Bring a list and stick with it. Take extra care at the checkout counter. That is where you are forced to stand and stare at the intriguing impulse items!

Stores are not designed to uplift your mood. Maybe that is because depressed shoppers spend more than happy shoppers. The researchers explain that when you're feeling sad, there is a higher degree of self-focus. And the combination of sadness and self-focus seems to impair spending judgment. Here is how to fight back: Do not "self-medicate" by going shopping when you feel sad, mad, or bored.

The "shopping experience" is designed to encourage you to spend more. They make it as easy as possible. They know that swiping a credit or debit card can almost seem like not paying at all. It feels way different than handing the cashier cold, hard cash and watching him put it in his drawer. Numerous studies show that people spend much more when they spend with a credit card. Here is how to fight back: Protect yourself from impulse spending by leaving your debit or credit card at home. Bring cash only and only the correct amount of cash.

Touching is dangerous. The "if you break it, you buy it" policy is a reality. There also is the danger of, "If you touch it, you may buy it." Stores are designed to make you want to stop and touch. There is something called the "endowment effect" that make you want to own what you touch. If you try it on, take it for a test drive, or sign up for the trial offer, you feel familiarity, connection, and ownership. Do not pick it up or "try it on for size" unless it fits in your spending allowance. If you cannot afford it, do not touch it!

Stores are designed to encourage you to buy more than you

planned. Here is how to fight back: If you only have a few items on your list, do not take a cart or bag when you enter the store. Sometimes a cart is inevitable. For example, when Heidi and her husband make their semi-annual pilgrimage to Costco, they each take one half of the list and a shopping cart. When they convene with their carts at the checkout line, apply the practice they call "cart cleanse." They put all the "needs" items in one of their two carts. The other cart holds the "wants" items. When they reach the cashier, they put the need items on the conveyor belt and tell the cashier, "Hi, we have x dollars, so please tell us just before you reach that amount." When the dollar amount is reached, they put all the unpurchased items back in the "wants" cart, say courteously, "Thank you, but we will buy these other things another time." Other shoppers nod with respect at their restraint. It takes discipline to shop at wholesale clubs, but this technique works like a charm.

Grocery stores make the food look appealing and tasty. Eat before you shop. Did you know that hunger makes you buy more? A 2009 study published in the Journal of Marketing Research showed that shoppers who ate a turkey and potatoes dinner before they shopped cut down on impulsive spending. Their dinner contained plenty of tryptophan, which synthesizes the neurotransmitter serotonin, which reduces impulsive behavior. The Pilgrims were not fools.

Be a gender-neutral shopper

Retailers know that women shop differently than men. Researchers say that men tend to be more focused at a store. Usually, they are at the store only to find what they need, pay for it, and leave. Women tend to appreciate the actual shopping experience. It may have something to do with ancient man going out to hunt the big game while the women gathered nuts and berries! In any case, smart retailers provide places to sit near the dressing rooms for dutiful husbands and boyfriends. Without the seating arrangement, customers would be dragged out of the store by their shopping partners much sooner. If you want to spend less time shopping, shop with someone who does not like to shop.

Here is further proof men and women are wired differently when it comes to shopping. According to a 2007 study in the *Journal of Personality and Social Psychology*, men were more likely to splurge on a luxury item after they were shown pictures of women. They also were more vulnerable to purchasing after they were touched on the arm by an attractive sales associate. Yes, "sex sells." Also, human touch releases oxytocin, a brain chemical linked to bonding and trust. Oxytocin has been shown to make people more generous with their money. Avoid oxytocin!

REAL LIFE CASE STUDY
"Making a Fresh Start with a New Attitude"
Written by *TheSmartestWay™* fan Lorie Towsley

A few years ago, I had the opportunity to become an assistant to a social media consultant. I made a point to try to learn everything he knew. Heidi attended one of his trainings and asked me for extra help. My boss agreed to let me help her. Soon he changed careers, and I decided to become a virtual assistant. I was becoming concerned about the stability of my marriage, and I wanted to be able to be able to create income while working from home, so I could help my three children do well in school and grow up without having to take on too much responsibility too soon.

I told Heidi that someday I was going to have my own virtual assistant agency, since I knew a ton of stay-at-home moms like myself who wanted to bring in extra money for their families. I created my own website and business cards, found a babysitter, and started going to networking meetings in town. Soon I had some clients who were small business owners. Eventually I had enough business to hire a few of my close friends. I had them sign an independent contractor contract with a non-compete clause. While I was training them in the easier tasks, I arranged for high-level, ongoing training and support for myself. That way, I will always have more knowledge than my employees. I raised my rate higher and hired a bookkeeper to keep track of invoicing and payroll.

Now that I have a reliable, core team of virtual assistants in place, I have started going after larger corporate clients, which I take care of personally. My preschooler started kindergarten recently, so now I have even more time to grow my business. I love having my own company, being my own boss, and setting my own hours around my kids' activities. If I can build my own company as a newly single mom with three school-age kids, I know that other moms can, too.

Here are a couple of my favorite tips for moms who want to save money at home:

- I plan ahead so I can buy things for my kids with CASH. I buy my kids clothes only two times a year, before summer and before school starts. Except for shoes, of course. I set aside CASH every month for their clothes. We get nothing at full price. If it is not on sale, they have to wait for it to go on sale. Also, I pay for Christmas in CASH. I set aside $20 for Christmas gifts from each month's paycheck. I buy cards and decorations at 75 percent off right after Christmas. I usually have all the cards mailed, the gifts wrapped, and the decorations up by the end of November. That way, I can focus on spending time with the kids during the holidays.

- I look for fun things to do with the kids that are FREE. We have "game nights" on Friday night, with movies and popcorn, and the kids invite their friends, so their parents *can go out for dinner. Then the parents help me with carpooling when I need to meet with clients. At Christmas time, we go to tree lightings, lighted house tours, and the snow to sled and make snowmen. We make inexpensive gifts with the kids' pictures and thumbprints on them. such as refrigerator magnets and coaster sets. We always have a cookie-swapping party, since baking cookies is inexpensive. As a single mom, I have found that what kids care about is if you are there for them. It's not how much stuff you buy them; it's how much time you spend with them that counts.*

Chapter 14

SAVING ON HOLIDAYS AND GIFTS

"We have three things in life to spend:
Time, energy, and money."

—Anonymous

A HOLIDAY HANGOVER is not a mandatory result of a "good" holiday. You can enjoy the holidays without fear of the January credit card bill nightmare. Here's how: Pay cash for everything this year and don't have any holiday debt! Then, the next year, put the equivalent amount into a holiday savings account. You will then have enough money for holiday gifts and there won't be a holiday credit card bill to pay off. Ask if your bank offers a Christmas club, or a plan that deducts automatically for holiday expenses.

The holiday season should be what you want it to be, not what everyone else wants it to be. Be adaptable; suggest options to achieve everyone's desires. If you want to see your family that lives far away, plan a summer reunion or celebrate a few weeks before or after Christmas when the airline rates are lower and the airports are less crowded. Avoid succumbing to holiday guilt that whispers in your ear that your gifts are not expensive enough or your house is not decorated enough. Also, refer to our first book's chapter on Gift Giving and Relationships.

Deck the halls

Be creative with "all the trimmings" of the season. Make your own wrapping paper from newspaper and magazine pages that you adorn with pretty ribbons. Revive old decorations by combining them and using them in new ways. Hang your greeting cards from a ribbon on a wall in the hall. Employ nature's decorations of pinecones, holly, poinsettia, and evergreens.

Consider buying an artificial tree instead of buying a new fresh tree every year. The artificial trees come in all sizes, shapes, and colors. They look remarkably lifelike and come in a variety of different kinds of trees, some with already-attached strings of lights.

Artificial trees cost less and save time shopping for a new tree each year. You don't have to remember to water it. You don't have to worry that it is a fire hazard. They are cleaner, with no sap or dropped needles.

If you miss the smell of fresh pine, which only lasts a few days anyway, light pine-scented candles from the dollar store. You can get steep discounts on artificial trees and Christmas lights right after Christmas at www.Michaels.com, www.HomeDepot.com, www.DoItCenter.com, and www.DecorStore.com.

Start a tradition

Start a tradition with your family. Talk to your family members about these ideas:

- Select a common theme for the gifts each year. For example, one year, all the gifts will be hand-made. The next year, all the gifts will be made from recycled materials. You can find hundreds of handmade items at www.Etsy.com. You can make pottery gifts at www.ColorMeMine.com. The average price range for a do-it-yourself pottery gift is under $20, including the studio fee and the kiln work of the piece.

- Start a gift jar. The whole family throws their coins into throughout the year. In December, take the jar to a coin-sorting machine and divide it up so everyone has their gift money for the holidays. Check www.CoinStar.com for details on change-counting machines near you. Since there is a percentage charge for counting the coins, it is better to have your children count the coins and put them into paper wrappers that you can get free of charge from your bank. You could also buy a coin sorter. You can ask the merchant teller at your bank if the bank provides other services to sort coins.

- Plan a family gift of volunteering in the community. Your family could donate their time wrapping gifts at local bookstores during the holidays to raise money for a specific non-profit organization that your family supports.

- Write thank you notes. This is the best way to be grateful and feel grateful. Heidi's mother started a family tradition when she was young that she still loves. Her mother divided the gift opening into two sessions. There was not always a lot under the tree, but the opening of each gift was given special attention. Each gift was opened one at a time, and everyone else watched while each gift was opened. On Christmas morning, they opened the gifts that they could give thanks for in person. On Christmas Eve, the prior evening, the family opened the gifts from everyone who would not be joining them on Christmas morning. Before they went to bed, a thank you note had been written for each of the gifts.

Be creative with gifts

Here are some ways to create gifts that will have significance and make memories:

- Create one spectacular handmade ornament each year for each member of the family. Make it signify a special accomplishment for that year, perhaps a little diploma ornament for the year that person graduated from high school or college or one with a sports theme for the athlete in the family.

- Give each other some kind of gift that includes photos. Some ideas for photo-related gifts are to apply photos or children's artwork using decoupage onto wooden or ceramic boxes, picture frames, ornaments, and coasters. You can order lots of products decorated with photos, such as blankets, mugs, and calendars. Put together a scrapbook of photos from last Christmas and give everyone a copy. Check out more options at www. SnapFish.com, www.costco.com, www.kinkos.com, www. ShutterFly.com, and www.walmart.com.

- Make a family-centered gift. Compile a family cookbook. Gather the family's favorite recipes and photos of the family in the kitchen and at the dining table. Put together a little book of Mom's Words of Wisdom or Dad's Favorite Sayings. If you are a budding videographer, you can make a short video of the family, say at the holidays this year, and give copies to everyone in your family next year. If you belong to a group or club, host an annual cookie recipe party; keep a master cookbook and album with recipes and photos of each year's party. You can put books together at sites such as www.SnapFish.com and www.ShutterFly.com.

Be creative with greeting cards

Make your own greeting cards. A special, handmade card can be a gift in itself. Handwrite a touching message inside and you have created a priceless memento. You may already have craft items at home or they can be bought very inexpensively at dollar stores. This is a fun project to do with children, too. Use recycled paper, wrapping paper, butcher paper. Get glue, scissors, colored markers, and a hole puncher. Glue on cut fabric pieces, silk flower petals, sequins, and gems. Through punched holes, weave raffia, satin cords, or ribbons to make designs such as a heart or birthday cake. Then close the card with a ribbon bow inserted through punched holes. You can glue together a custom-sized envelope or buy a packet of colored envelopes and make your cards the size to fit inside the envelopes.

Find inspiration at card stores. Heidi saves the store-bought cards she receives and recycles them by cutting out pieces and redesigning them on her own creations. You can even make a gift of a boxed set of custom cards. Include a variety of card topics, such as get well cards, birthday cards, thank you cards, and congratulations cards. If the gift is for someone who recently had a baby and they know lots of others who are having babies soon, a box full of baby congratulations cards would be a welcome gift. Your gift of a packet of cards can be delivered in a fabric bag you sewed from remnant fabric pieces, or you can decorate a box to hold the cards. In this age of emailing cards and shopping online for gifts, a personal touch is more welcome than ever.

Try re-gifting

Have you ever "re-given" a gift you received, but did not need or want? Sam kept a record of things that he'd received over the previous year as gifts from clients, relatives, or friends, and found that over 50 percent of them were things that he did not need. That is not to say that he does not like gifts! He repackages or gives away those gifts. While he appreciated the thought behind them, it is best to thank the giver and give the item to those who can use them. Be sure to re-gift carefully and avoid embarrassment by remembering who gave which gift to you. They must never find out that you gave it to someone else!

Here's another "guilty secret" about re-gifting. You can give a charitable donation in the recipient's name in lieu of a gift. Then you can get a tax deduction for the donation if you itemize your taxes! Before you pursue this option, be sure that the recipient would appreciate your donation gift in their name. First, though, make sure that a "real" gift is not preferable. Pick a charity that the recipient has a heart for. Here is a blended option: charities that let gift card recipients chose where the money goes, such as www.CharityGiftCertificates.org, www. JustGive.org, and www.TisBest.org.

Give gifts that really matter

As we've discussed in our first book, gifts of time or that show personal thought or attention are valued the most and often more than those that are expensive. The simplest most direct way of solving this problem is to ask, whenever possible, directly from the recipient what they need from you or want most from you. When that is not possible, the question should be directed to someone who knows them well, preferably a significant other, a close relative, or business associate.

There are a number of things to consider when making a gift:
a. Is it appropriate?
b. Will it be something you can afford?
c. What sort of a message does the gift tell the giver?

Are you sending a gift because of respect and care for the person who is to receive it, or to show off and make a statement about yourself?

Show that you care about the receiver's preferences and needs. You may find the perfect gift online. Save time and wait for a bargain. Getting the best deal can take vigilance. Just stick to that one special gift item you are looking for.

When picking out a gift for your employer, make sure that it is not too expensive. That would send the wrong message and does wrong to your wallet, too. Also, don't choose a gift that is too personal, such as clothing, toiletries, or jewelry. Give the gift at the office, not outside the office.

Giving gifts to charity

Some parents are trying to teach their children early on that they do not have to go insane about gifts and parties, as seen by the two mothers that started www.echoage.com. Echoage provides an opportunity for your children to give a donation to the organization in lieu of the money they would have spent on a gift for you.

Another trend is department stores partnering with designers and offering to donate a percentage of all proceeds from sales of their clothes within a specific timeframe to a specific charity. An example is the sale of Ralph Lauren children's clothes at Bloomingdale's going toward a music center. At www. GoodShop.com, you can link to the sites of 1,400 retailers and up to 30 percent of what you spend will be donated to your favorite charity. Good Search www.GoodSearch.com is a search engine that donates a penny to your favorite charity for every online search you make. These are great ideas for great causes.

Instead of the annual day-long gift-opening extravaganza that no one can really afford, consider this idea: The entire family can chip in the amount of their normal gift budget and instead buy something really significant for a needy family overseas. Gifts that count for these people are chickens, cows, goats, or other livestock that can sustain them. Above all, pick a charity that is legitimate, such as www.CharityNavigator.com, www. Kiva.com, www.DonorsChoose.com, and www.ModestNeeds. com. More and more people are resolving to restore sanity to holiday shopping by vowing to spend half as much on gifts and twice as much on giving to worthy causes.

The gift of your time is a no-cost present, and yet it is very valuable. For example, Sam has found that his grandchildren, in their high school and college years, appreciate and benefit from sitting down with him and discussing their life plans. They need this advice far more than they need an expensive Apple product.

Avoid store gift cards

Small gifts related to a person's preferences show you have taken the time to determine their interests. A simple gift that is personalized will often have a greater impact than one that is more elaborate. You can often learn from friends what your recipient wants or needs. Tying the gift to a need or personal interest means more than the price of the gift.

The credit card reform bill of 2009 prohibits gift cards from expiring in less than five years and prohibits fees if a card is used within the first year. When you give a gift card, remind the recipient of these "three secrets" to gift card success: 1. Head to the store and use them and not store them away. 2. Keep track of how much is left on the card. 3. After the card is drained of funds, keep it until you are sure you are not going to return any of the items you purchased. Some retailers will not accept a return without the gift card. Gift cards can be easy to give, but frustrating to use.

Nevertheless, retailers love them. Gift cards give retailers the benefit of the "float" on your money. In 2009 alone, consumers lost nearly $8 billion because of unredeemed, lost, or expired gift cards according to TowerGroup, a research firm owned by MasterCard. This situation has not gone unnoticed by cash-strapped states. The next year, New Jersey attempted to claim almost $80 million annually by expanding its authority to seize funds from unused travelers' checks and gift cards. Apparently, $20 here and $50 there can add up.

The problem with gift cards

Here are some more of our objections to gift cards:

- They sit in the recipient's wallet, saying "You need to go shopping at x store." Stealth marketing at its best.

- What if your recipient does not even like shopping? (Is there such a person?) They might appreciate it if you do the shopping for them.

- Electronic gift cards are super-convenient, but what if the recipient is not comfortable with shopping online?

- You need to know the insider information on the health of the company. In a shaky economy, many stores close, but they usually do not give shoppers prior notice. If the retailer you choose goes out of business, all or part of the value of the gift card may not be honored. Gift card holders are considered uninsured creditors. This was the case with Bombay Co. and Sharper Image when they went out of business. Consumer Reports estimated that unused Sharper Image gift cards totaled $20 million. In this scenario, you are not only embarrassed, you may find yourself feeling obligated to also buy a replacement gift!

- In 2011, consumers spent nearly $25 billion on gift cards. More than 75 percent of shoppers purchased one or more gift cards during the Christmas holiday. Stores are making a fortune off of gift cards. Since so many of them go unredeemed (good for the retailer; bad for the consumer), some states are pursuing dormant cards to boost state revenue. Note the recurring theme of "unused gift cards." Again, good for the retailers; bad for the consumer.

- Gift cards train kids to become accustomed to using plastic money instead of cash.

- Your recipient will probably spend their own money on the gift you gave them. In a Consumer Reports survey, 65 percent of respondents said they typically spend more than the value of the gift card. Heidi once received a free $10 gift card with purchase that could only be redeemed a month later. When she returned to the store, she found nothing to buy that was less than $10. Rather than walk out in disgust, she shelled out her own money to pay for the balance for an item she did not need. All that because she had made the effort to return to the store and she did not want to leave empty handed, even though she felt like a fool.

The problem with "open-loop" gift cards

We recommend caution with reloadable, prepaid debit cards. Sometimes they are referred to as "open-loop" gift cards. They are issued by credit card companies and they look like a credit card. They can be used at a variety of retailers, but do not assume that they can be used just anywhere. They can be loaded and reloaded with funds. Unfortunately, they come loaded with an assortment of fees that can rapidly erode the balance. There is a fee for the first purchase, monthly fees, ATM withdrawal fees, reloading fees, replacement fees, and our favorite, inactivity fees. We love it that you pay a fee if you use it and you pay a fee if you don't! If you are not careful, soon you could be giving a gift with a negative balance! This can end up with an embarrassing moment at the cash register! Some prepaid cards charge "shortage" fees of nearly $30. That means that you owe *them* if you spend more money than the amount stored on the card! The notion of gift card convenience is ludicrous.

If you must give this kind of card, you should feel obligated to try to decipher the fine print on the card and inform your recipient of the restrictions and fees. Otherwise, they could have a very negative "buying experience," and at worst, resent you for causing them the trouble or embarrassment.

These kinds of cards do have some applicable uses, but not as gifts. For example, the federal government is using them to return refunds to some taxpayers who do not have checking accounts. Taxpayers may be paying for all the fees, but that is a separate topic altogether.

Want to know what we really think about gift cards?

As we wrote in our anti-gift card rant in our first book, gift cards are convenient to buy and give. However, they aren't very thoughtful. Instead of giving money and letting the receiver choose where to use the money, they require the user to go to a specific retailer. Oh, but money isn't very personal, you say? Why is a gift card more personal than money, really?

We have to agree with Judith Martin, known as Miss Manners, who says gift cards are "a pathetic compromise convenient to people who do not trust their judgment about selecting the right present for those whose taste they ought to know." Suffice to say, the financial services industry sees nothing wrong with prepaid debit cards. Apparently neither do lots of time-and-consideration-challenged gift givers. The total amount of these cards is expected to exceed a mind-boggling $440 billion by 2017, four times the estimated value in 2009 according to independent research commissioned by MasterCard. Like your mother used to say, "Just because everyone else is doing it does not mean you should, too."

Furthermore, gift cards make retailers money in so many ways. For example, a few years ago for Christmas, Heidi received a gift card to a coffee shop chain. You know, the coffee shop with locations on every street corner in America. She seldom drinks coffee, so the card sat in her wallet as a reminder, "I need to go there sometime." Finally, she managed to almost use the card up. Eighty cents remained on the card. When she tried to buy a cup of coffee with it, she was told that the card had too little money on it to qualify to be used. So she had to pay for the coffee, even though she had planned on not doing so. She felt resentful, like she was being "nickeled and dimed" by the system. Sure, it's a small amount, but those small amounts add up dramatically for the retailer. Needless to say, despite our criticism, the popularity of gift cards flourishes.

Pamper yourself

To get free gifts for yourself, all you have to do is be willing to spend a few minutes online and divulge your birth date. (Do not give the accurate year, as that is too much information for your security.) You can register with sites like www. BirthdayFreebies.com and learn about all the birthday freebie opportunities in your area. Check out www.ProBargainHunter. com, www.savings.com, and www.FreebieSecretsMag.com for birthday giveaways. There is no reason to go hungry—or pay a dime for food—on your birthday. Restaurants know that you will not celebrate alone and your friends will pay full price! You can get a free dessert or free food on your birthday if you sign up for the "birthday clubs" at Outback Steakhouse www.outback.com, TGI Fridays www.tgiFridays. com, Red Lobster www.RedLobster.com, Olive Garden www. OliveGarden.com, Applebee's www.Applebees.com, Chili's www.chilis.com, Baskin Robbins www.BaskinRobbins.com, Buca di Beppo www.Bucadibeppo.com, Cold Stone Creamery www.ColdStoneCreamery.com, and at one of Sam's all-time favorites, Home Town Buffet www.HomeTownbuffet.com. At Chevy's www.Chevys.com you also receive a free sombrero for your birthday.

You can get a free meal for your birthday at several restaurant chains, including Denny's www.Dennys.com, Fuddrucker's www.fuddruckers.com, and International House of Pancakes www.ihop.com.

Look also online for retailers that offer discounts via birthday clubs, such as Kmart www.kmart.com. A couture women's clothing shop in Heidi's area gives a discount for the entire month of their customers' birthdays—and offers to call the customers' husbands and remind them of that fact.

Don't give gifts that send the wrong message

Recent events have made us extremely conscious of situations where a gift sends the wrong message. The first involves a business executive. While she makes a good salary which has enabled her to acquire a home, she is a single mother with a college-age son and a daughter attending a prestigious high school in a very expensive neighborhood. She has sacrificed and worked hard for her son and daughter to get a good education.

Her daughter recently reached driving age. The mother bought her daughter a luxury car that cost approximately forty thousand dollars. She reasoned that she had to do it "because other kids in the high school have that kind of car given to them by their parents." This is a typical example of trying to keep up with the Joneses at the cost of real values. The mother instead could have bought her daughter a less expensive car and started a college fund for her. That would give her the long-term benefit of a lifetime of earning power versus the short-term benefit of appearing to look affluent in her high school parking lot.

Now the mother will be stuck with making payments on a car she will not own at the end of the payment period. Even if she can afford to make the payments, she will be in real jeopardy if at any time in the future she loses her job. Instead of having reserves which can help see the family through financial reversals, the mother placed her future income in jeopardy, all for a "want" (her daughter to have an expensive car) rather than a "need" (modest, but adequate transportation).

On the other hand, Sam knows a wealthy mother and father who sent their son off to college with the least expensive, full-size car they could find, even though they have higher income than the mother of the daughter in the previous example. The car cost less than $20,000 new and they had him earn part of the purchase price. This couple has always followed the principals of never buying anything that they couldn't pay cash for and postponing their wants until they could fulfill them comfortably within their existing resources and not go into debt.

As we often say throughout our books, gifts that are given for "show" are more for the giver's pleasure. On the other hand, gifts that represent values, such as education and security, express more concern for the recipient. This is a difficult concept for many to get used to, particularly if they have not been taught these principals by their parents.

REAL LIFE CASE STUDY
"Redefining Retirement"
Written by *TheSmartestWay*™ fan Richard Fletcher

Let me tell you about some dumb attitudes that have almost stopped me from saving money for when I will need it most.

When I was in high school, I needed to start saving money for college. My sister was heading for college, so she offered me her afterschool typing job. At first, I had a dumb attitude: "I can't take that job because I don't know how to type, and I don't have time to learn how to type or to take a typing class." Then I replaced my dumb attitude with a smart attitude: "I'll learn how to type somehow, because I really need the money!"

My sister borrowed a typing book and I taught myself to type by applying the seat of my pants to a chair and my fingers to her portable typewriter. (It didn't hurt that I played piano.)

I got the job, saved my wages, paid my dental bills, and bought my first car for $75. It was a cute Ford Model A that was as old as I was, 18 years old. The top speed without rattling was 50 mph, which was a safe speed for highways back then. I was now a "young man about town," all because I took the time to learn how to type.

Later in my life, I found that I had to again reject a dumb attitude about saving in exchange for a smart attitude. With my education credentials and previous lifestyle, this has required a conscious adjustment. Here's how I do it: Instead of telling myself that I don't have enough money to buy what I want, I tell myself that I do have enough money for what I need. I'm never without money because I keep the same large bill in my wallet. Then when I get "the wants" for something I don't need, I can pass it up by CHOICE, and not because "I don't have enough money."

My bank account defines how I feel about myself and my worth as a person. I express my self-respect by tithing to myself each month. I see how long I can keep from spending those funds, knowing I'm entitled to spend it all by the end of the month, if I choose.

I shouldn't have to get all my furniture in a thrift store. But that's where I bought an elegant, white brocade, almost-new sleeper sofa for $50. I decided to take advantage of "senior's savings day," since after all, I am a senior. I returned to the thrift store on seniors' savings day and bought my sofa for 50 percent off!

In this economy, there are deals to be had, so be sure to negotiate, negotiate, negotiate. The sellers are motivated. It is a buyers' market. Now I am a happy saver, and every once in a while, a happy buyer.

Chapter 15

SAVING ON PARTIES AND ENTERTAINMENT

"Wealth is the ability to fully experience life."
—Henry David Thoreau

I F YOU LIKE TO ENTERTAIN or gather groups of friends together, there are creative ways to have a lot of fun without spending a lot!

If you have an idea for a party, but are short on time, send invitations out via email. Email invitation websites such as www. evite.com, offer attractive, free invitations for a wide variety of social gatherings, everything from birthday parties and holiday parties to GNOs (girls' night out/guys' night out) and potluck dinners. Also, the system collects RSVP responses, so you spend less time answering responses on the phone. Our first book has a chapter on Entertainment that you would enjoy, too.

Heidi uses these kinds of online invitations for meeting friends at happy hours at jazz lounges, lectures and concerts at museums, and picnics and concerts in the park. Everything is better with friends along, so why not send out an evite whenever you schedule something fun on your calendar?

With this kind of casual "Come if you can" type of gathering, your friends will pay their own admission and buy their own food and beverages. There is no upfront cost for you, the event planner. If a few friends can't show up, other friends will bring new friends, and you are still going to have a good time.

No matter where you meet your friends for your parties and social gatherings, set aside a specific amount of money to be spent at the event. Make a list of what you want to spend during the event and be very specific. How much money do you expect to need to buy drinks, food, gifts, gas, parking, event tickets, taxis, or new clothes? One way to cut back is to limit the number of drinks you buy, or better yet, volunteer to be the designated driver, and the bar often will give you non-alcoholic drinks for free.

Commit to only spending that amount and put that amount in cash in an envelope to take with you. You will make adjustments as you go along, so keep a running total on the envelope. When the envelope is empty, stop spending. You will enjoy yourself more if you know you can afford it.

Entertaining at home

If you like to entertain at home, any time is a good time to rev up the barbeque or light the candles you have been saving for a "special occasion." Heidi's opinion on parties, entertainment, and fun with friends is, "If not now… when?"

For home parties, spend time, not money, presenting with flair. Decorate serving trays with fresh edible greenery such as mint, rosemary, curly parsley. To save money on alcohol, you can create a signature punch that enhances the theme of your party. Tie napkins and utensils with ribbon and a little message on a tiny note card. Borrow whatever serving pieces you need.

For dessert, you can bake a cake yourself, rather than buying it. Keep it simple, such as a huge cookie cake. You can find friends of friends who like to make party cakes, or inquire at the local community college if there is a culinary arts department.

You can even start a supper club, a monthly dinner party that is a fancy version of potluck. The host family for that month selects the menu from a culinary magazine. You can name the party after the magazine. For example, if you use Gourmet Magazine, it could be called the Gourmet Group. The host family provides the entrée and the other families bring the rest of the items on the menu.

Other ideas are themed parties, such as a wine tasting party or a dessert party, and have each guest bring a bottle of wine or a dessert. Game night is fun, with just few friends learning a new card game or a larger group playing old-fashioned games, such as Twister or charades. A fun Halloween theme is homemade costumes. The rule is that the costume can be made only with things you already own. Or they can be thrift store-only costumes. If it is a birthday, bat mitzvah, bar mitzvah, sweet sixteen, quineanera, or anniversary party, let the honored person chose his or her colors and theme. You can find more party game ideas at www.PartyGameIdeas.com and www.BirthdayPartyIdeas.com.

If you want to get your friends together, but your home is not the best place, find another comfortable, inexpensive location. The quality of your friends makes the event special, not the quality of the venue where you get together with them.

Keep your party high on creativity and low on expense

One drain on the party budget is decorations, so get creative. Centerpieces can be reusable if they consist of silk flowers or non-perishable decorative materials. They can be designed with edibles, such as fruit, decorated cookies, or colorful candies. To avoid misunderstandings about who should be allowed to take the centerpieces home, have a simple contest and the winner at each table gets the centerpiece of that table. For example, tape a random number between 1 and 50 on the bottom of each centerpiece. The person at the table who selects the closest number wins.

A rainbow circles party is a fun, inexpensive theme for little boys' or girls' birthday parties. Everyone wears polka dots on their clothes. For appetizers, you can serve orange slices, cantaloupe balls, watermelon balls, Melba toast rounds and crackers, and round slices of cheese. For lunch, you can serve pepperoni pizza and salad with mozzarella cheese balls and cherry tomatoes. The cake can be decorated with rainbow colored M&Ms and candy confetti. Buy a bubble-making machine or bubble-shooting guns at www.ToysRUs.com. Decorate your walls with large paper circles in bright, primary colors. Cover the invitations and cups and plates with sticky dots from the office supply stores. Have balloons on ribbons hung from the ceiling. For toddlers, buy armloads of small plastic balls to fill up a kid-sized swimming pool.

Enjoy culture at museums

Some museums, observatories, and botanical gardens offer a free day once a week or once a month. Have you explored all the museums in your community? When you travel, do you check out the museums in new cities? Search for all the available museum resources at the Chamber of Commerce Visitor's Center and website, newspapers, and college community calendars listings. Fantastic free museums are the Smithsonian in Washington, D.C. and its branches, such as in New York City. If you live in New York City, Friday is the free day for museums, including Museum of Modern Art and the Guggenheim Museum.

If you live in or visit the Los Angeles area, there is a bounty of museum freebies. The Getty Museum in Brentwood is open every day with free admission and just $15 per car for parking for the entire day. The Los Angeles County Museum of Art and the Norton Simon Museum in Pasadena (seen around the world on New Year's Day as the backdrop for the Rose Parade) are open to the public at no charge on certain days of the month. For each museum, find the specific times on the museum's websites.

Exhibits at libraries, art galleries, colleges, and universities are free. Colleges and universities have faculty recitals and senior recitals, lectures, presentations and readings, and student drama performances. Check out cultural centers and historical societies, which often do not charge admission.

Have fun at home

There are lots of fun activities to do at home with friends and family. You can play board games and card games, complete a jigsaw puzzles, build a fort with blankets or a large appliance box, run in the sprinklers, wash the dog, blow bubbles, create a collage with finger paints and found objects, make masks by covering a balloon with paper mache, learn magic tricks online, or just lie on the grass and gaze at the clouds or the stars and build a long fairy tale together. For movies, rent from Redbox www.RedBox.com or www.Netflix.com, or swap favorite DVDs. You can also find inexpensive movies at libraries and thrift stores.

If you are alone, you can write a budget, a will, a list of your goals, or a letter of advice to your children. You can do a bill reduction inventory, try a new recipe, or bake some healthy casseroles that will save you time and money during the week, organize your media collection or your bookshelf, do some deep cleaning or home repair projects, take a long bath or a nap, meditate, practice yoga positions, learn a musical instrument, write a journal entry or poetry, start a new a hobby, write a thank you or thinking of you note, or clip coupons. You can even clean out your desk, closets, attic, or the garage and prepare for a yard sale.

On your computer, find a video on www.YouTube.com about your favorite hobby, find a blog or podcast you like and read or listen to the archives, listen to music on www.Pandora.com

or www.last.fm, choose a tutorial on MIT's open courseware, study a foreign language tutorial, scan your family photos into your hard drive, or research a fantasy trip to an exotic location. You can also explore freeware at www.openoffice.com and www.scribes.com, learn how to create mind maps with www.mindmeister.com, or start researching your family tree on www.ancestry.com.

Have fun close to home outdoors

You don't have to go far from home to find entertainment. Most stadiums offer deep discounts for the "cheap" seats. Check out the map to see if anything would be obstructing your view. Sometimes you get a better view of the full scope of the game while sitting in the middle or even upper deck seats. Even with bad seats, you can roam the public places in the stadium. Check out www.StubHub.com, www.GoldStar.com, and www.TicketsNow.com. Tickets for minor league games are less expensive. Check out www.minorleaguebaseball.com.

Theme parks offer deep discounts, such as an annual pass when you buy one regular admission. You can find theme park discount tickets at grocery stores and through your local AAA office. The YMCA offers inexpensive swimming, sports, and camping trips. Libraries have summer programs, book groups, and film nights. Attend free community classes. Participate at a workshop at the local hardware store.

Community festivals and music festival information is at www.FestivalFinder.com. The Chambers of Commerce and City Community Centers will have information on expos, fairs, and festivals in your area. Also search online for activities in your community. Does your area have a winery that offers tours and tastings? What about a local manufacturing facility or factory that offers tours?

You can go hiking in nearby national parks. Check out www.nps.gov/findapark and www.stateparks.com/usa.html. Speaking of taking long walks, how about exploring your city's historic district? Many cities offer a free walking tour of historic architecture. Contact your local conservancy. If you live near a public pond, pack a basket lunch, rent a row boat, and while away, spend a contemplative hour on the water. If you live near the ocean, plan a day at the beach to collect shells. At the park, play soccer or Frisbee, have a picnic, bring binoculars and watch the birds, and collect rocks or leaves.

Have fun close to home indoors

You can save money on movies by going to a matinee, which is the first showing. Check out independent theaters, and try the drive-in movies. If you have lots of family members or you cannot live without movies, AMC Theatres and Cinemark offer tickets in bulk at www.bulktix.com. To avoid paying the fees charged by online ticket reservation websites, go to the theater extra early when there are no lines and then go out to eat after the movie.

When you go to the movies, you don't want to get stuck with outrageous parking garage fees. Remember to validate your parking ticket. Watch the restrictions about when the first free hours are. At one popular mall in the Los Angeles area, a mere one minute over the time limit can equal an additional $7 in fees. If you are going to be at the mall for a while, say for dinner and a movie, have dinner, then go back to the car, drive around the block and re-enter the parking garage to get additional free parking.

If you are a true movie fan, you could consider getting a part-time job at the local movie theater. If you love Broadway shows, consider signing up for www.TicketWatch.com for discounts. If you love drama and music, at the beginning of the summer, go online to find the dates of all the free outdoor concerts and plays in your area and neighboring areas. Put them on your calendar.

At large, outdoor amphitheaters, the lawn seats are less expensive. Some online ticket distributors help theaters, concert halls, and clubs in major cities get rid of unsold seats at a discount. Go to www.GoldStar.com and www.StubHub.com. Find a consolidated ticket booth in your area. Ask your local hometown theater or concert hall if they would allow you to sit in on rehearsals for no charge, or buy tickets at a discount just before showtime. Volunteer to pass out playbills or help in concession stand during intermission. Find free live music at coffeehouses and bars.

Learn a new hobby

Do you really know how to use that camera or camcorder you bought a few years ago? What about other electronics and sports equipment that is sitting around the house? Use and enjoy what you already have.

If you want to try a new hobby, start with used, rented, or borrowed equipment. Ask a friend to teach you or take a few inexpensive lessons at the community college. Try before you buy. A potentially lucrative hobby is furniture refinishing. If you have a garage and/or sewing machine, you can learn to make slipcovers or buff up thrift store furniture and resell it at consignment stores, or perhaps give as gifts. Quilting, knitting, and crocheting are also potentially lucrative hobbies. Look on www.freecycle.com for raw materials that you can use to create things that are salable. If you make jewelry out of "found" and recycled objects, you can sell them at the online crafts marketplace www.etsy.com, where more than 200,000 merchants sell handmade goods.

Don't overspend on hobby equipment. First find out if you love the hobby and are willing to put in the time, money, and patience to become good at it. For costly hobbies, first rent your equipment, then buy good quality, but used, things.

If you are interested in exploring golf, you need to understand that expensive golf clubs will not automatically make you a good golfer. You can start playing at the municipal golf course by renting the equipment and taking lessons there. You can buy used golf clubs on www.amazon.com or www.ebay.com. The clone brands cost less. You can find golf coupons and more information at www.FrugalGolfer.com. You can find cheap golf balls at sporting good stores. If you find that you have become passionate about the game of golf, consider offering your services as a part-time caddy or work at the local golf shop.

Some people find that their favorite hobby is to volunteer. Visit someone you know who is confined to their home. Bring some flowers or baked goods and offer to run errands, do some repairs, or clean their house. You can also check out www.volunteermatch.org.

REAL LIFE CASE STUDY
"College Nightlife Tips"
Written by *TheSmartestWay*™ fan Jonathan Young

A big part of the college experience is the nightlife. Finally out of the constraints of parental control, students often tend to let loose. Subsequently, their funds do the same thing. I noticed that many students put more emphasize on their weekends than their schoolwork. They need to learn to enjoy their time away from their books without losing the money to pay for them!

Once students reach the legal drinking age, new doors are open to them—and those doors often lead right to the bars! When I was in college, I enjoyed going out with a group of friends, but I realized how often my bank account regretted it in the morning.

Here are a few simple tricks that helped me save cash when I went out on the town during my college years. These tips can help any student.

• It is easy to get caught up in the atmosphere of the bar scene. Don't feel obligated to buy expensive drinks. I don't

know how many times I saw students try to woo friends with a fancy drink. You are in college—everyone is broke!

- *If you're with a group, buy a pitcher of beer. You can usually get one for under $7.00, which is much cheaper than buying individual drafts.*
- *Buy the first pitcher. I've noticed after a few drinks, your group will become more generous with their funds and more likely try to outspend the first buyer.*
- *Find special deals. College bars are always offering deals for students to entice them in.*
- *Leave the credit card at home. Bars have expensive minimum tabs on credit cards, and people often feel like they have infinite money with the plastic. I've found that carrying only cash helped give me a better sense of how much I was spending.*
- *Have a drink before you leave. Split a cheap six-pack with friends in your dorm, so you don't go to the watering hole thirsty.*
- *There are other great nightlife activities in college that don't involve alcohol. Concerts on campus are always reasonably priced and usually feature popular artists. Go to "open-mic" nights, speakers, and movies on campus. Not only is it a great way to save a buck, but it's a great way to meet new people.*

Students should experience everything college has to offer, but they do not have to fall behind financially to do so. It's easy to get caught up spending a lot in college, so students need to realize that there are other options. They can have fun and still be financially responsible without making major changes to their lifestyle.

Chapter 16

SAM'S PRINCIPLES OF FINANCIAL INDEPENDENCE — Part II

It's not what you make;
it's what you make of yourself.

—Samuel K. Freshman

NOTE: Part I of Sam's Principles can be found in our first book, ***TheSmartestWay™ to Save.***

1. Don't buy a new or replacement item until you've paid for the last one. Paying for two items at the same time can set back your goals.
2. Never rely on promises, windfalls, or inheritances. Your lifestyle should be based on your actual, recurring income.
3. A transaction is not complete until the money is in your bank account. What can go wrong often will.
4. If you are expecting to receive extra money, plan for it in advance. Do not waste it, but commit it toward debt reduction, investments, and things of lasting value and utility.
5. Don't be "penny wise and pound foolish." For example, don't drive a longer distance to save money on gas, when the cost of getting there exceeds the savings.

6. Time is money. Everyone needs balance in their life. Plan your time to monetize it so that you're either improving your financial situation, moving yourself toward your financial goals, improving your skills and education, or improving your personal relationships.

7. Your most important resource is your health. Pay attention to it and give it priority. Remember the old adage, "An ounce of prevention is worth a pound of cure."

8. Understand your addictions and weaknesses. Admit them to yourself, get help where you need it, and develop plans and techniques to avoid them.

9. Visualize your goals. Be sure they are achievable, objective, and measurable. Think about your savings habits constantly.

10. Accomplish at least one act every day that carries you toward your goals. The safe and sure way to financial independence is to get there one step at a time.

11. Learn to think in alternatives. Is there something you can do that will be satisfactory for your goal, but will cost much less than what you were planning to spend?

12. Learn to shop on sale days and at clearance sales. Almost every retailer has periodic sales. Find out when your favorite stores have sales.

13. Be familiar with all of the pre-owned merchandise stores in your area. Learn what each has to offer and how often the merchandise changes.

14. Become familiar with bartering. Offer to exchange your services or surplus goods for those goods or services you need.

15. Use generic and "house" or store brands wherever there are major savings. Try generic and house brands of drugs, cosmetics, and many grocery items. Check labels and ingredients to compare.

16. Buy amounts appropriate for your use. If you use a lot of something, the largest size you can afford may give

you great savings. If it is something you use very seldom, a smaller size is probably a better investment. If you use a lot, stock up; otherwise, don't.

17. Determine when to buy and when to rent. Consider buying anything you intend to keep and use often. For example, the cost of used furniture is often not much more than a few months' rent on new furniture. If you're using something on only a few occasions, borrow it (preferable) or rent it. There is no reason to keep capital tied up in things you do not use.

18. Maximize your living arrangement. Sharing a home or apartment can result in great savings on your single biggest expense.

19. Maximize your ride. Do you and your partner both need a car, or can one of you rideshare to work? Transportation is often the second largest expense after your residence. Some couples can manage with one car if they live near public transportation or can arrange to ride-share. In some cases, people in metropolitan areas do not need to own a car at all.

20. "Act as if." Incorporate your new behaviors in your life naturally. Think of the old adage, "Fake it till you make it." Act as if your saving habits are already a regular part of your life. Soon they will be.

21. Find an excellent role model. Imitate that person. Ask your successful friends what their savings habits are and how they save.

22. Maximize your associations. Associate with people who are successful savers and investors. Avoid people who tend to encourage you to break your saving habits or who criticize your new savings plans. Remember the phrase, "Birds of a feather flock together." Attract the people who will help, not harm you.

23. Attitude is more important than aptitude. A positive attitude will get you further in life than all the training in

the world. You may know how to save, but you will not save until you want to. So have a positive attitude about saving, get started, and learn as you go!

24. Maximize your income. You get more money by making more money or by spending less. It's easier to spend less than to make more.

25. If you are a renter, rent by the month, not by the week. The difference in your total outlay may be dramatic. If the savings are worth it, make the sacrifices necessary to get the deposit together for a monthly lease. If you can lease for 12 months, sometimes landlords will give you a month or two rent-free.

26. Double-up wherever you can. You may not need both a landline and a cell phone, as many find only a cell phone is more than adequate.

27. Never quit your present job until you have a replacement. It is much easier to get hired if you are employed when you apply. Gaps in employment are looked on with disfavor by employers.

28. With respect to major items, such as refrigerators or cars, compare the cost of repair versus the cost to replace. Maybe you can put something in "like new" condition for less than the replacement cost.

29. Understand what is wrong with credit cards. If you don't control your use of them, they encourage you to buy things you do not need, with money you do not have, to impress people you should not be trying to impress.

REAL LIFE CASE STUDY
"Cutting Back on a Medical School Budget —
Part Three"
Written by *TheSmartestWay*™ fan Rebecca Rubin

- When my husband was in medical school, it was very expensive, but we managed to keep a low overhead on our spending. What helped us stick to our saving goals was not to view the changes we made in our lifestyle as a limitation or setback. Living on a limited budget forced us to be more creative, and also to be more detail oriented and aware of ourselves. We sat down together and itemized everything we did and spent. We didn't purchase anything for our apartment without talking to one another about it first. This prevented us from buying the same thing twice or ending up with something unnecessary. We knew what we could spend after taxes, and we thought about what we wanted and needed. We tried to find a balance between both, while living within our means and saving money.

- When we researched potential apartments to rent, we looked to live in neighborhoods very close to where we work. This saved money on gas for the commute, and we didn't add extra mileage to our cars. When we searched for apartments, we asked the landlord what the monthly utilities were and if parking were included. We chose our apartment because it reduced our commute to work. It was renovated with new appliances and it was the nicest one we'd found within the parameters of our budget. It also included two parking spaces at no additional charge, which weren't included in the other apartments we looked at.

- It was also equally important for us to live in walking distance to all of our essential errands and a couple of restaurants we like. We were able to save money on gas when we ran our errands. We lived across the street from a post office and in walking distance from a grocery store, *the farmers' market every Sunday, the pharmacy, the dry cleaners, and a place for coffee. When we first moved, we went to all the dry cleaners in the area to see which was the best value and also did a good job. We ultimately saved hundreds of dollars because of our initial research.*

- *We didn't have cable TV. We watched movies we rented from the library and through Netflix. Cable is something we choose to live without to save money and give us time to spend on other activities. Living without cable saved us about $500 a year. It was definitely a lifestyle change. Ultimately, we were more productive and spent less time in front of the TV.*

- *We were on the same cellular phone carriers as our families who live outside of our calling zones. We planned ahead to call friends who aren't on our calling plan during times when the minutes are free. We never dialed 411 for information or directions; there is an extra dollar or more cost for such information, and this can accumulate to a large phone bill. We had a toll free information service plugged into our speed dial that serves the same purpose as 411. We also blocked text messaging from our phones. This prevented us from getting charged additional costs. We always looked carefully at the phone bill so as to catch any mistakes.*

- *We always kept spare change in our car, because putting money in the meter is a lot less than paying the cost of a ticket. When possible, we tried to arrive early to restaurants and event, so we could find the best parking rate, rather than be obligated to valet park. We also contested the ticket if it was given out unjustly. My husband once received a parking ticket when he was called into the hospital for an emergency, had to work overnight, and wasn't even parked illegally. As a result, the fine was lifted.*

- *We only subscribed to essential magazines. For example, my husband needs to read the New England Journal of Medicine, so he reads it free online through UCLA.*

Fortunately, most of the publications I read as a resource are free or online. We also read magazines and the **New York Times** *online. My husband chose to limit magazines from the budget, but he chose to keep satellite radio, which he loves, in his car. He canceled his subscription to the* **New Yorker,** *and we check it out from the local library.*

- *We shopped at the farmers' market where the produce is significantly less expensive than many grocery stores, and we shopped at Trader Joe's for other food items. We tried to plan our meals in advance, and we never went to the store without a list or when we were hungry. Because we tried to limit ourselves on going out to eat, and I love to cook, we liked to make nice home cooked meals trying new recipes within a reasonable budget. Because we ate well at home, it wasn't as necessary to go out to eat. We also had two basil plants and a tomato plant, which saved us money on those items.*

- *For wedding and baby shower gifts, we often gave homemade gifts or a nice picture frame with a photo of a good memory. Weddings and parties for people we love were hard for us to attend if we had to travel. We were invited to 10 weddings and three baby showers one year! One was even in Colombia! We attended when we could and if we had the time off from work. If the wedding was not possible to attend, we would try to attend the shower. When we went to the wedding, we booked rooms with the best rates if we couldn't stay with friends or family.*

- *We took a lot of advice from people who have more experience than we do in how to save money. And we tried to find role models who have weathered tough financial times and come out successfully and who are not overly burdened by their financial situation. We kept sight of what we were saving for, both in the long term and short term. In the short term, we wanted to have the security of having money saved in case of an emergency. Keeping our goals in mind helped us to live frugally.*

SUGGESTED READING

COOKBOOKS

Better Homes & Garden Budget Meals,
  Better Homes and Gardens
Betty Crocker Money Saving Meals, Betty Crocker
Eat Healthy on a Budget, Elizabeth Martyn
Family Feasts for $75 a Week, Mary Ostyn
Feast for a Farthing, Molly Finn
Five Meals for $5, Jaci Rae and Albert Garcia
Fix, Freeze, Feast, Kati Neville and Lindsay Tkacsik
Fix-it and Forget-it 5-ingredient Favorites,
  Comforting Slow Cooker Recipes,
  Phyllis Pellman Good
Healthy Meals for Less: Great Tasting, Simple Recipes
  for Under $1 per Serving, Jonni McCoy
Living More With Less and More With Less Cookbook,
  Doris Janzen Longacre
Money-Saving Meals, Sandra Lee
Once A Month Cooking, Mimi Wilson
  and Mary Beth Lagerborg
One Hundred Meals for $ 5 or Less, Jennifer Maughan
Pillsbury the Savvy Shopper's Cookbook, Pillsbury Editors
Quick Thrifty Cooking
Semi-Homemade Slow Cooking, Sandra Lee
Seventy Meals, One Trip to the Store Cookbook,
  Kelly Donlea
Taste vs. Fat: How to Save Money, Time and
  Your Taste Buds, Elaine Magee
Ten Dollar Dinner, Melissa D'Arabian
The $5 Dinner Mom Cookbook, Erin Chase
The $50 Dinner Party, Sally Sampson
The $7 a Meal Slow Cooker Cookbook, Linda Larson
The Frugal Foodie Cookbook, Lynette Rohrer Shirk
The Frugal Gourmet, Jeff Smith

The Organized Kitchen, Brett Sember
The Thrifty Cookbook, Lucy Doncaster
Vegan on the Cheap, Robin Robertson

COUPONS

20 Grocery Store Savings Ideas, Tammie Taylor
Beyond Extreme Couponing, Whitney Simon
Coupon Millionaire, Nadine Brown
Coupon Savings Guide, John Lewis
Couponing Secrets, Vivian Boettcher
Cut It Out and Start Saving, Denise Long
"Cut it Out" How I Feed My Family 19 Ten, Kate Megill
Don't Throw Those Coupons Away
    Everyday Coupon Book, Amy Nichols
Greatest Secrets of the Coupon Mom, Stephanie Nelson
Joyful Momma's Guide to Shopping
    and Cooking Frugally, Kimberly Eddy
Super Shop Like the Coupon Queen, Susan Samtur
The Coupon Mom's Guide to Cutting Your
    Grocery Bills in Half, Stephanie Nelson
The Couponizer, Amy Bergin
The Lazy Couponer, Jamie Chase

ENERGY SAVINGS

Consumer Guide to Home Energy Savings,
    Jennifer Thorney Amann
Cut Your Energy Bills Now, Bruce Haley
DIY Solar Projects, Eric W. Smith
Energy Savers: Tips on Saving Energy and Money
    at Home, U.S. Dept. of Energy
Homemade Money: How to Save Energy and Dollars
    in Your Home, H. Richard Heede
How to Really Save Money and Energy on Cooling
    Your Home, George Barton

How to Save Energy and Lower Your Electric Bills,
Sarah Lilton
How to Solar Power Your Home, Martha Maeda
Living Green, Marvin Equin
The Energy Efficient Home, Mark Walker
The Home Energy Diet, Paul Scheckel

FREE STUFF AND GOOD DEALS

Bargain Hunter's Handbook, Andrew Adamides
Bargain Junkie, Annie Korzen Digest
**Free Money, Free Stuff: The Select Guide to Public
and Private Deals, Steals & Giveaways,** Reader's
Free Stuff and Bargains for Seniors,
the Editors of FC&A Publishing
Good Housekeeping Good Deals, Editors of
Good Housekeeping
How to Haggle, Max Edison
How to Shop for Free, Kathy Spencer and Samantha Rose
Instant Bargains, Kimberly Panger
**Never Pay Retail Again, Shop Smart, Spend Less,
and Look Your Best Ever,** Daisy Lewellyn
The Best Free Things for Seniors, Linda and Bob Kalian
**The Cheapskate Next Door: The Surprising Secrets
of Americans Living Happily
Below Their Means,** Jeff Yeager
Wow! You Saved How Much? Renita R. Perrone

GARDENING

Easy Lawn & Garden Care, Maureen Gilmer
Gardening When It Counts In Hard Times,
Steve Solomon
Grow Great Grub, Gayla Trail
Homegrown Vegetables, Jim Wilson

Homesteading: A Back to Basics Guide to Growing Your Own Food, Abigail Gehring

How to Grow Your Own Vegetables, Michael Kressy

Mini-Framing, Brett Markham

One Magic Square, Lolo-Houbein

Small Plot, Big Harvest, DK Publishing

Small Plot, High Yield Gardening, Sal Gilberti and Larry Sheehan

The Everything Grow Your Own Vegetable Book, Catherine Abbott

The Frugal Gardener, Catriona Tudor Erier

The Green Thumb Book, George Abraham

The Ultimate Guide to Growing Your Own Food, Monte Burch

The Year-Round Vegetable Gardener, Nikki Jabbour

Vegetable Gardening 101, Kathy Burns-Millard

Vegetable Gardening For Dummies, Charlie Nardozzi

GROCERY SHOPPING

101 Ways to Save Money and Energy in Your Grocery Store, Dave Troesh

Beating the High Cost of Eating, Barbara Salsbury

Beating the High Cost of Eating, Barbara Salsbury and Simmons Sandi

Better Groceries for Less Cash, Randall Putala

Big Little Guide to Save Money Grocery Shopping, Melissa McCann

Coupon Mom's Guide to Cutting Your Grocery Bills in Half, Stephanie Nelson

Cut Your Grocery Bill in Half, Steve Economides and Annette Economides

Easy Ways to Save Money on Groceries Without Clipping Coupons, Alice Simon

Eat Well, Spend Less, Sarah Fowler

Grocery Savings, June Locker

How to Save Money on Grocery Shopping, Quick Easy Guides and Instant Bargains, Kimberly Danger
Instant Bargains, Kimberly Danger
Money Saving on Your Grocery Bill, William Harbin
Pick Another Checkout Lane, Honey: Save Big Money and Make the Grocery Aisle Your Catwalk, Joanie Demer and Heather Wheeler
Save Money on Every Trip to the Grocery Store, Eric Summers
Save Your Money, Save Your Family, Toni Touse
Shop Smart, Save More: Learn the Grocery Game and Save Hundreds of Dollars a Month, Teri Gault
Stop-Wasting Money, Carol Coots
The Elite Grocery Shopper, Raymond Reitand
Twenty Grocery Store Savings Ideas, Tammy Taylor

HOLIDAYS AND GIFTS

Debt-Proof the Holidays, Mary Hunt
Fast Fabric Gifts, Sally Southern
Finding the Perfect Gift, Huloana and Preston
Hundred Dollar Holiday, Bill McKibben
The Homemade Home: 5 Thrifty and Chic Handmade Projects, Sania Pell
Unplug the Christmas Machine: A Complete Guide to Putting Love and Joy Back Into the Season, Jo Robinson
Your Christmas, 100 Ways to Reduce the Stress and Recapture the Joy of the Holidays, Elaine St. James

MONEY IN YOUR LIFE

Give it Up! My Year of Learning to Live Better With Less, Mary Carlomango
It's Not About Money, Brent Kessel
Money and the Meaning of Life, Jacob Needleman
Money Well Spent, Wallace Curiel

On Desire: Why We Want What We Want,
   William B. Irvine
Sound Health Sound Wealth, Luanne Oakes, Ph.D
The Problem with Money, Jane Honeck
The Secret Meaning of Money, Cloe Madanes
The Seven Stages of Money Maturity:
   Understanding the Spirit and Value of Money
   In Your Life, George Kinder
The Soul of Money: Recharging Your Inner Resources,
   Lynne Twist and Teresa Barker
What Your Money Means and How to Use It Well,
   Frank Hanna
Your Money or Your Life, Vicki Robin

SAVINGS TIPS

1,001 Things They Won't Tell You: An Insider's Guide
   to Spending, Saving and Living Wisely, Jonathan Dahl
   and the Editors of *Smart Money Magazine*
10,001 Ways to Live Large on a Small Budget,
   the Writers of Wise Bread
365 Ways to Live Cheap: Your Everyday Guide to
   Saving Money, Trent Hamm
573 Ways to Save, Peter Sander and Jennifer Sander
600 Simple Tips to Save You Money, John Nardini
66 Ways to Save Money Today, Consumer Literary
   Consortium and Jon Sullivan
92 Easy Ways to Save Money, S.P. Vernon
A Tip a Day with Ellie Kay, Ellie Kay
Absolutely Amazing Ways to Save Money
   on Everything, James Paris
All About Money, Larry Burkett
Amazing Insider Secrets: 1703 Money Saving Tips,
   Jeff Bredenberg
Be Centsable, Chrissy Pate

Better Living, Tips for Saving Time and Money,
Sherri Brennen

Cheaper: Insider's Tips for Saving on Everything,
Rick Doble

Easy Ways to Save Money Every Month, A.C. Jones

Everyday Cheapskate's Greatest Tips, Mary Hunt,
Running Press, 2005.

Frugal Living, Kevin Anderson

**Healthy, Wealthy, and Wise: 1001 Money-Saving
Secrets to Curb Your Spending, Clear Up
Financial Chaos, Improve Your Health,
and Make Your Life Easier!**
The Editors of FC&A Publishing

How to Save Money Every Day on Everything,
Andrea Stein

How to Save Money Everyday, Ellie Kay

Life on a Budget, Mookey Mae Phillips

Making the Most of Your Money Now,
Jane Bryant Quinn

Save Big: Cut Your Top Five Costs, Elisabeth Leamy

Saving Money With the Tightwad Twins, Anne Fox
and Susan Fox

Savings Savvy, Kelly Hancock

Simple Tips to Save Money, Anna Biligan

**The 77 Secrets of How to Live Your Life Happy,
Healthy, Wealthy and Wise,** Allen Jesson

**The Beardstown Ladies' Guide to Smart Spending
for Big Savings,** The Beardstown Ladies' Investment
Club With Robin Dellabough

The Frugal Senior, Rich Gray

The Guide to Frugal Living, Jack Forenger

Thrifty: Living the Frugal Life with Style,
Margorie Harris

Twenty Amazingly Simple Ways to Save,
Augustine Mwanje

SHOPPING

Bogo—Buy One, Get One Free! Martin Sloane
Brand Sense, Martin Lindstrom
Buyology, Martin Lindstrom
Cheap Online Shopping: A Beginner's Guide,
    Carol Spykes
Never Pay Retail, How to Save 20% to 80%
    on Everything You Buy, Ed. Sid Kirchheimer
Online Shopper's Survival Guide, Jacquelyn Lynn
Retail Hell, Freeman Hall
Shop for a Day with Jaci Rae: How to Get Almost
    Anything Free, Jaci Rae
The Best of Online Shopping, Lisa and Jonathan Price
The Costco Experience, Larry Gerston
The Frugal Shopper, Penny Lopez

SHOPPING FOR CLOTHES

How to Be a Budget Fashionista, Kathyrn Finney
How to Be a Teen Fashionista: Put Together the
    Hottest Outfits and Accessories on any Budget,
    Chase Koopersmith
How to Save Money on Buying Clothes, Quick
    and Easy Guides
My Year Without Clothes Shopping, Jill Chivers
Save Money Thrift and Consignment Clothes
    Shopping, Sandi Lynn
Style on a Shoestring, Andy Paige
The Shop Smart Girls Consignment and Thrift Stores
    Shopping Guide, S Girl
Virtual Vintage: The Insider's Guide to Buying
    and Selling Fashion Online, Linda Lindroth
    and Deborah Newell Tornello

SIMPLICITY

'Tis a Gift to Be Simple, Barbara Sorenson
**Celebrate Simply: Your Guide to Simpler,
    More Meaningful Holidays,** Nancy Twigg
**Get Satisfied, How Twenty People Like You Found the
    Satisfaction of Enough,** Ed. Carol Holst
How Much is Enough?, Arun Abbey and Andrew Ford
Inner Simplicity, Elaine St. James
Living Your Life for Half the Price Without Sacrifice,
    Mary Hunt
Secrets of Simplicity, Learn to Live Better with Less,
    Mary Carlomagno
Simple Abundance, Sarah Ban Breathnach
Simplify Your Life With Kids, Elaine St. James
Simplify Your Life, Elaine St. James
**The Happy Minimalist: Financial Independence,
    Good Health and A Better Planet for Us All,**
    Peter Lawrence
The Simple Guide to a Minimalist Life, Leo Buata
**Voluntary Simplicity: Toward a Way of Life That Is
    Outwardly Simple, Inwardly Rich,** (2nd Ed.),
    Duane Elgin

THRIFTINESS AND FRUGALITY

Be Thrifty: How to Live Better With Less, Pia Cation
    and Califia Suntree
Frugal Living for Dummies, Deborah Taylor-Hough
**Frugallionaire—500 Fabulous Ways to Live Richly and
    Save a Fortune,** Francine Jaskiewicz
How to Be Frugal, Brian Carr
Suddenly Frugal, Leah Ingram
Teach Yourself Thrifty Living, Barty Phillips
**The New Frugality, How to Consume Less, Save More,
    and Live Better,** Chris Farrell

The Thrift Book: Live Well and Spend Less, India Knight
**The Tightwad Gazette I, II, and III, Promoting
    Thrift as a Virtue,** Amy Daczyn
Thrifty Living: the Frugal Life with Style,
    Marjorie Harris

NOTE: More books for suggested reading are listed
        in our first book.

ABOUT THE AUTHORS

SAM FRESHMAN

Sam Freshman, a Stanford-educated attorney, is also a real estate developer, banker, business owner, investor, lecturer, author, and professor. His company, Standard Management Co., manages more than $400 million of real estate assets and business enterprises. His book, ***"Principles of Real Estate Syndication,"*** is considered the landmark work on the subject. Clients pay up to $5,000 for his customized workshops and personal coaching on behavioral attitudes that create success. See www.standardmanagement.com and www.syndicationideas.com.

HEIDI CLINGEN

Heidi Clingen has been a journalist, editor, and writer for the past 25 years, including positions at Apparel News Group and The Wall Street Journal, where she received a Dow Jones Foundation fellowship. Heidi earned a bachelor's degree in journalism from San Francisco State University, and a screenwriting certificate from UCLA. She devotes her time to researching and speaking on how to live well on a modest income.

WE OFFER COACHING!

We offer workshops, seminars, and training programs for groups of all ages and sizes, as well as one-on-one coaching sessions. Contact us at Heidi@TheSmartestWay.com to tell us how we can help!

**ALSO BY SAMUEL K. FRESHMAN
AND HEIDI E. CLINGEN**

*TheSmartestWay™ to Save
Why You Can't Hang on to Money
and What to Do About It*

ALSO BY SAMUEL K. FRESHMAN
*Principles of Real Estate Syndication
with Entertainment and Oil-Gas Syndication
Supplements*
3rd Edition

These books are available at
**www.Amazon.com,
www.BarnesandNoble.com,**
and your local bookstore.

WANT TO INVEST YOUR SAVINGS? READ THIS BOOK!

Principles of Real Estate Syndication
(3rd Edition)

By Samuel K. Freshman

Known throughout the real estate industry as the definitive how-to guide, ***Principles of Real Estate Syndication*** is filled with examples and illustrations of all aspects of buying property with others. This reference guide thoroughly explains the theory and practice of this time-honored way to invest in real estate. Here are some of the many comments posted about this book on Amazon:

"...This book could be titled, how to build a real estate empire. The book provides practical information and advice on avoiding common mistakes..."

"...Comprehensive and authoritative, a must-read for anyone who contemplates investing in a syndication or becoming a syndicator... A treasure trove of information...."

"...A hands-on book, well-written, easy to comprehend, and offers the reader a strategic insight into a complex business form... Should be a permanent fixture in every office..."

"...This is the instruction manual for this type of venture—a compelling synthesis of practical and technical advice and legal analysis. I recommend the book to anyone involved in real estate or other syndications—attorneys, accountants, bankers, investors, syndicators, students, and more."

"...If you are serious about making money in real estate, read this book. ...This book explains in simple and easy-to-understand language the preparation, execution, and practices that must be taken to become successful in the field..."

"...I truly believe this book, if properly followed, can make anybody who reads it substantial amounts of money..."

"...There are dozens of real estate investing books out there, but this is clearly the best I've found..."

Sam has a distinguished career in real estate and law, as an advisor, developer, and investment partner. He is chairman of Stanford Professionals in Real Estate (SPIRE). He is past Chairman of the Legal and Accounting Committee of the California Real Estate Association Syndication Division. He assisted in the preparation of the California Corporation and Real Estate Commissioner's syndicate regulations. In 1961, he formed Standard Management Co., which has sponsored hundreds of millions of dollars of investments in real estate projects throughout the country.

You can purchase ***Principles of Real Estate Syndication,*** 3rd Edition at your local bookstore, on Amazon.com, or on syndicationideas.com.

HOW YOU CAN GET INVOLVED!

HELP US LAUNCH
TheSmartestWay™ Project!

Many worthwhile organizations have asked us for help with financial literacy training. As a result, we are establishing **TheSmartestWay™ Project** to make our savings books available at cost to qualified organizations that operate homeless shelters, battered women shelters, food pantries, and inner-city schools, as well as financial literacy programs at banks and credit unions. It is our intention that our books, educational programs, and our good will can help adults and teens who are struggling financially. We invite you to contact us at Heidi@TheSmartestWay.com about programs that you would like to receive our books.

TELL US YOUR STORY!

We were proud to share all the stories and essays that the readers of our first book sent in! Now, we would love to hear YOUR story about how you save money! If you email us at Heidi@TheSmartestWay.com a brief, 500 word essay, we will be delighted to include it In our upcoming third book, TheSmartestWay™ to Save Big, The Large Things in Life for Less. Please join our expanding community of sensational savers. We look forward to hearing from all of you!

RECEIVE OUR NEWSLETTER!

Sign up for our newsletter filled with tips, stories, and sug-gestions by emailing us at
Heidi@TheSmartestWay.com or
clicking on the signup box on our website at
www TheSmartestWay.com!

MORE PRAISE FOR
TheSmartestWay™ to Save
Why You Can't Hang Onto Money
and What to Do About It

"This is powerful! As a banker for the past 25 years, I believe that people need to go back to basics these days. This book is entertaining, offers good value, and is a book you even want to go back and reread! I want to share it with young people who are going out in the world, so they can start their financial life in the right direction."

—Oscar Dominguez
Vice President and Group Manager, Union Bank of California

"I found this book to be very straightforward and filled with a lot of common sense, which is very refreshing at this point in time."

—Sally Stahl
Director MBA Career Counseling and Education
UCLA Anderson School of Management

"In this uncertain economy, we're all looking for ways to cut expenses and put money in the bank. This book makes it easier. It is all about saving techniques, not investments--don't spend to keep up with others, think before you spend, pay yourself first, comparison show, and avoid debt."

—Alice Berger

"In this most critical time in our economy, so many are struggling with finances and really need this book. I've read many such books, but this one is surprisingly enjoyable, with great quotes and short stories to hold your interest, even put a little smile on your face. It has the most extensive list of resources I've found anywhere, to help in debt assistance, financial planning, and saving money on everything you can imagine. I have copied Sam's list and hung it on my wall to review daily. Grab a copy of this right away, as well as a couple more for family and friends!"

—Lisa Berg
Artist

"This book is the gold standard of financial guides. It has cogent, commonsensical, comprehensive ways to save money and plan for the future. The information is easily accessible. The arguments are persuasive. The vision is easy to see. The writing is outstanding, which is rare for books in this field. This is a fine book which has made a profound difference in my spending and savings patterns. I highly recommend it, particularly to people like me who need extra effort to save."

—John Shosky, Ph.D.
Professor at American University

"If I had known when I was young the techniques in this book, I would have done things a lot differently and surely would be in a more comfortable financial position during my retirement. But, alas, I didn't read this book until I was 70. And you can be sure I am much smarter now. Thanks, Sam Freshman and Heidi Clingen. By putting these ideas into effect, I feel confident I won't outlive my money!"

—Calista Lee Brown

"I want to give thanks for the tips and inspirations that **TheSmartestWay™** to Save gave me. I finished the book in a week and a half because it was very inspirational and exciting to read. I was looking for ways to save money so as I was browsing on Amazon, I noticed the high number of good reviews, which led me to purchase your book. After reading the book, it occurred to me that I've been wasting too much money on materialistic things such as shoes and clothes. As a result, I've become more alert on my spending and have set up automatic weekly savings account distributions. I hope many others will come to discover and learn from the many helpful tips in your first and upcoming books."

—Jin Rong
Aerospace Design Engineer

"I've read other books on money management, but they all produced such guilt and distress that I felt sure that my family could never apply their principles to achieve financial stability. This book offers compassionate encouragement, coupled with sound financial advice that has freed me from the shame and anxiety that has held me captive for decades. This book has empowered me to conquer not only my fear, but also my failure. I now know how to stop the bleeding."

—Sue Molenda
Actress and Screenwriter

"What I like best about this book is its ability to keep matters on a level that is easy to understand. This sounds simple enough, but many financial books stray too far and use complex financial terminology, graphs, amortization tables, and other things that will likely go beyond the understanding of the Average Joe, the very type of person these books are usually intended to assist. Another quality that I like about this book is the authors' ability to help show ways to save money without going to extremes. Most of the advice offered in TheSmartestWay™ to Save is sound, reasonable, and easy to implement. We are a consumer-driven society and many of us do, indeed, spend more than we should, often on things we don't need or even want all that badly. This book offers a good, quick way to discover different ways to save and different ways to implement changes to spending habits, improve net worth, and live a more worry-free life. It's a very practical book that can benefit anyone who reads it and takes its advice to heart."

—Bryan Carey
Amazon Top 500 Reviewer
and Owner of www.MoneySavingParent.com

"These are things we all should know. Yet, somewhere along the way, we forgot or perhaps just quieted the voice inside that tried to keep us out of spending trouble. The goal is to save as much as you can, be smart about what you do spend, and enjoy life, knowing your finances are in your control and not controlling you. This book is highly recommended for those wanting financial freedom and the knowledge on how to get it done."

—Mary Nichelson
Blogger

"Thank you for writing the book! I graduated with a degree in Entrepreneurial Business with a minor in economics and my university didn't cover half the information on personal finance that you guys did. I've already put a lot of changes in place and got a budget set up for the first time. I graduated in 2008 with a business degree and my university didn't cover half the information on personal finance that you guys did. I'm getting my student loans paid off and investing the rest in myself first! Thanks again for writing the book and helping me implement these changes!"

—Steve Staten
Credit Union Board Member

"This book consolidates all we know, knew, or should know about our relationship to our money. Like common sense, the fiscal responsibility in our times is relatively rare. When I am tempted to say, "Oh, I know this," it is wise to acknowledge that, "I don't do this." This book codifies the givens of successful financial habits. My favorite quotes here are, 'If you don't understand your relationship to money, you can't control,' and 'Credit is very, very expensive money.'"

—Sally Berg
Retired Teacher

"Of all the books I've read on saving, this book is so personal and direct that it holds my attention best. Then it nails me to the wall with my particular money worries and habits, where I can see them sometimes for the first time. Example: I've actually watched my self-image rise and fall with my bank account. This book has given me many alternatives to that habit, among others. It fairly sparkles with brilliant, short paragraphs, divulging personal examples in a rare combination of brevity and warmth. It helped my niece a lot in getting her fiscal act together when she was in trouble, so her parents thank you, too."

—Richard Fletcher, Ph.D.

"This book will be very helpful for readers of all ages. Throughout the book, the authors effectively balance the psychological features of spending and saving, along with some practical tips for creating financial independence. I found the book to be clear, concise and to the point. Once I started reading the book I couldn't put it down until I READ IT from cover to cover. I can't wait to read the sequel to this book!
—Irene S. Roth
Book Reviewer

"This book gives great practical financial advice. It is the perfect guide for the challenges faced during these tough economic times. I recommend it as a guide for every household."
—Carl Goldman
Radio Station Owner

"If you use 'shopping strategies' to buy clothes, you can become a smart shopper. Here are two more ideas for saving money on clothes: you can put them on hold or use the "ten question list" in the book."
—Joelle Lum
Sixth Grader

"I can't begin to tell you what a positive impact your book has made to my economic life! Now when I stand in front of the item I just HAVE to have, I ask myself "is it a need or a want?" Nine out of ten times, I can walk away. I no longer use my credit card as a revolving charge. When I purchase using my credit card, I make sure I am able to pay it off at the end of the month and no longer have to pay the additional interest. After putting your plan into action, I actually end up with money at the end of the month! I am able to save for all the Christmas gifts I want to purchase and pay cash for them at the time of purchase! Thank you for the sound and simple advice!"
—Sue Baxter
Marketing Executive

INDEX

10 Question Test: 111

Allowance: 96, 142

Bad habits: 31-34

Bartering: xviii, 174

Benefits of savings: 55-56

Charity: 59-61, 112, 152-153

Closets: 38, 119, 167

Clothes: 16, 18, 42, 56, 61, 63, 89-91, 93-94, 97-111, 123, 140, 145, 153, 164, 166, 187, 200

Clothes diet: 120-121

College: xviii, 6, 9, 52-53, 74, 78, 122, 133-134, 140-141, 150, 154, 159-172

Color: 90-95, 112-113, 117, 139-140, 142, 148, 155, 166

Consignment stores: 101-104, 107, 170

Coupons: 2, 52, 68-70, 100, 105, 109, 118-119, 127-131, 167, 171, 181, 183

Credit cards: xviii, 8, 18, 23, 32, 40, 96-97, 172, 177

Creativity: 16, 34, 55, 91, 93, 95, 130, 165

Debt: xviii, 2, 6, 13-17, 22-23, 37, 40, 50-51, 96, 104, 108, 147, 160, 173, 184, 196

Debt addiction: 15, 17

Discount: 2, 52, 68-70, 74-75, 82, 93, 99-101, 105, 118, 127-130, 135, 140, 148, 159-170

Discount stores: 2, 75, 101, 140

Electronics: 15, 108, 137, 170

Entertainment: 6, 45, 48, 86, 119, 128, 141, 163, 163-171

Exercise: 3, 43, 56, 62, 109, 140

Fashion: 7, 37, 48, 89, 90-96, 101-108, 112-113, 116-117, 120-121, 165, 187

Fast food: 57, 85-86, 129-130

Financial independence: 32, 37, 45, 50, 173-175, 179, 188, 200

Financial literacy: 8-9, 38, 195

Food: xviii, 3, 5, 18, 35, 52-53, 58-60, 67-87, 109, 129, 131-132, 136, 158, 164, 180, 183, 194

Food calendar: 71

Frugality: xviii, 1, 2, 41, 49, 188

Fun: 11, 14-16, 48, 75, 100, 112, 119, 141, 145, 151, 163-169, 172

Goal setting: 35-36

Gardening: 75, 67, 182-183

Gift cards: 7, 58, 154-158

Gifts: 22, 33, 59, 61, 98, 115, 145-161, 164, 170, 179, 184, 200

Good habits: 29, 32-34

Greetings cards: 148, 150

Grocery shopping: 67-68, 72-74, 182-184

Grooming: 138-139

Heidi: xviii, 16, 32, 41, 68, 74, 76, 82-94, 100-120, 129-133, 140-149, 156-159, 163, 190-191, 194, 196

Hobbies: 4, 11, 56, 138, 170

Holidays: 145, 147-161, 184, 188

Libraries: 141, 167, 168

Meals: 52-53, 71-72, 84, 86, 109, 179-180

Money style: 21-27

Museums: 31, 130, 163, 166

Needs: 17, 34-37, 42-58, 76, 96, 105,
    108, 114, 123, 139-140, 143,
    152-154, 174, 179

Online shopping: 117-118, 187

Outlets: 74, 99, 106

Parties: 48, 121, 153, 163-171, 179

Pre-used: 104

Principles of Financial Independence:
    173

Principles of Real Estate Syndication:
    190-193

Re-gifting: 151-152

Restaurants: 16, 25-26, 31, 33, 53, 59,
    127-134, 158, 178-179

Retirement: 2-8, 46, 61, 69, 160, 196

Sales: 2, 40, 63, 75, 83, 98, 101-104,
    116-119, 144, 153, 174

Sam: xvii, 30, 40, 43, 51, 56, 61, 67, 72,
    83, 98, 107, 128, 133, 141, 151, 153,
    158, 160, 173, 179, 190-193, 196

Savers secrets: 43-53

Self-care: 61-62

Shopping: xvii, xviii, 2-3, 6-8, 16-17,
    22, 44, 48, 52, 55-58, 63, 67-78, 82,
    85, 90, 93, 95, 99, 110, 117-121, 130,
    142-144, 148, 151, 153, 155, 181,
    183-184, 187, 200

Spending: xvii, 1-7, 13-18, 22-28, 33-34,
    39, 40-49, 56, 58, 62, 96, 97-99, 107,
    111, 118, 123, 135-136, 142-145,
    161, 163-164, 172, 176-177
    185-186, 196-198, 200

Thrift shops: 103

Thriftiness: 188

Value: xix, 1-5, 16-17, 26, 30-33, 43,
    50-53, 69, 99, 107, 131-137,
    152-160, 172, 178, 185, 195

Visualizing: 36, 38

Wants: 34, 36, 37, 42, 50, 57, 116, 143,
    147, 154, 160, 161

Women: 4, 7, 48-49, 72, 89, 91-95, 107,
    115, 139, 143, 144, 159, 194